most loved recipe collection most loved recipe collection most loved recipe collection

most loved

Company's Coming®

Treats

most loved recipe collection by Jean Paré

most loved

Treats

Pictured on Divider:
Candy Bar Squares, page 92

We gratefully acknowledge the following suppliers for their generous support of our Test and Photography Kitchens:

Corelle®
Hamilton Beach® Canada
Lagostina®
Proctor Silex® Canada
Tupperware®

Our special thanks to the following businesses for providing props for photography:

Anchor Hocking Canada
Canhome Global
Casa Bugatti
Cherison Enterprises Inc.
Danesco Inc.
Island Pottery Inc.
Klass Works
Linens 'N Things
Michaels The Arts And Crafts Store
Mikasa Home Store
Pfaltzgraff Canada
Pier 1 Imports
Stokes
The Royal Doulton Store
Zellers

Pictured from left: Chocolate Orange Cake, page 6; Swedish Tea Cakes, page 34; Nanaimo Bars, page 72; Mars Bars Squares, page 74; Bocconne Dolce, page 52.

table of contents

the Company's Coming story

"never share a recipe you wouldn't use yourself"

Jean Paré (pronounced "jeen PAIR-ee") grew up understanding that the combination of family, friends and home cooking is the best recipe for a good life. From her mother, she learned to appreciate good cooking, while her father praised even her earliest attempts in the kitchen. When Jean left home, she took with her a love of cooking, many family recipes and an intriguing desire to read cookbooks as if they were novels!

In 1963, when her four children had all reached school age, Jean volunteered to cater the 50th Anniversary of the Vermilion School of Agriculture, now Lakeland College, in Alberta, Canada. Working out of her home, Jean prepared a dinner for more than 1,000 people, which launched a flourishing catering operation that continued for over 18 years. During that time, she had countless opportunities to test new ideas with immediate feedback—resulting in empty plates and contented customers! Whether preparing cocktail sandwiches for a house party or serving a hot meal for 1,500 people, Jean Paré earned a reputation for good food, courteous service and reasonable prices.

As requests for her recipes mounted, Jean was often asked the question, "Why don't you write a cookbook?" Jean responded by teaming up with her son, Grant Lovig, in the fall of 1980 to form Company's Coming Publishing Limited. The publication of *150 Delicious Squares* on April 14, 1981 marked the debut of what would soon become one of the world's most popular cookbook series.

The company has grown since those early days when Jean worked from a spare bedroom in her home. Today, she continues to write recipes while working closely with the staff of the Recipe Factory, as the Company's Coming test kitchen is affectionately known. There she fills the role of mentor, assisting with the development of recipes people most want to use for everyday cooking and easy entertaining. Every Company's Coming recipe is *kitchen-tested* before it's approved for publication.

Jean's daughter, Gail Lovig, is responsible for marketing and distribution, leading a team that includes sales personnel located in major cities across Canada. In addition, Company's Coming cookbooks are published and distributed under licence in the United States, Australia and other world markets. Bestsellers many times over in English, Company's Coming cookbooks have also been published in French and Spanish.

Familiar and trusted in home kitchens around the world, Company's Coming cookbooks are offered in a variety of formats. Highly regarded as kitchen workbooks, the softcover Original Series, with its lay-flat plastic comb binding, is still a favourite among readers.

Jean Paré's approach to cooking has always called for *quick and easy recipes* using *everyday ingredients*. That view has served her well. The recipient of many awards, including the Queen Elizabeth Golden Jubilee medal, Jean was appointed a Member of the Order of Canada, her country's highest lifetime achievement honour.

Jean continues to gain new supporters by adhering to what she calls The Golden Rule of Cooking: *"Never share a recipe you wouldn't use yourself."* It's an approach that works— *millions of times over!*

foreword

Most Loved Treats is the third volume in our Most Loved Recipe Collection and is especially compiled to satisfy your sweet tooth. Whether you crave something quick and delicious to top off your supper or something slow and sweet to linger over with coffee or tea, you're sure to find the perfect treat among these time-honoured favourites. Every recipe is easy to follow and uses common ingredients you most likely have on hand, but results in extraordinary treats you didn't know you could make at home. Try it! You'll find you can almost taste that first bite with your eyes!

Dessert is the grand finale at mealtime. I usually follow a heavier meal with a light dessert, but I go all out with dessert if the meal is lighter. To help you choose just the right treat for the occasion, we've organized the recipes in this book into five convenient sections. You'll find every recipe photographed in scrumptious colour. When you have some extra time to spend in the kitchen, select something from the Cakes & Cheesecakes section to show off your culinary skills. When you have the urge to bake something soft, chocolate or nutty for snacking, Cookies has just what you need. Looking for a more substantial treat? Try any one of our delightful Desserts. The section on Squares, Bars & Brownies is stacked full of bite-size bliss, and Sweet Snacks is filled with those oh-so-tempting favourites you just can't do without.

Want something extra special to complete the tasty treat you've just made? Why not display it to full advantage on a brightly coloured serving plate or on delicate china? Add fruit garnishes or chocolate curls and you're all set for company! And remember, the next treat you make could become your newest family tradition—because the best part of making something sweet is sharing it with those you love.

With this superb collection of *Most Loved Treats*, you'll never be at a loss when company's coming, even if it's only a company of one—you!

Jean Paré

nutrition information

Each recipe has been analyzed using the most up-to-date version of the Canadian Nutrient File from Health Canada, which is based on the United States Department of Agriculture (USDA) Nutrient Data Base. If more than one ingredient is listed (such as "hard margarine or butter"), or a range is given (1 – 2 tsp., 5 – 10 mL) then the first ingredient or amount is used in the analysis. Where an ingredient reads "sprinkle," "optional," or "for garnish," it is not included as part of the nutrition information. Milk, unless stated otherwise, is 1% and cooking oil, unless stated otherwise, is canola.

Margaret Ng, B.Sc. (Hon), M.A.
Registered Dietitian

Milk chocolate flavour with a splash of orange. A delicious dessert to serve any time.

Chocolate Orange Cake

Hard margarine (or butter), softened	1/2 cup	125 mL
Granulated sugar	3/4 cup	175 mL
Large eggs	2	2
Orange flavouring	2 tsp.	10 mL
Semi-sweet chocolate baking squares (1 oz., 28 g, each), chopped	3	3
Sour milk (see Note)	3/4 cup	175 mL
All-purpose flour	2 cups	500 mL
Baking soda	1 tsp.	5 mL
Salt	1/2 tsp.	2 mL
CHOCOLATE ORANGE ICING		
Icing (confectioner's) sugar	4 cups	1 L
Block of cream cheese, softened	8 oz.	250 g
Cocoa, sifted if lumpy	1/2 cup	125 mL
Hard margarine (or butter), softened	1/4 cup	60 mL
Orange flavouring	2 tsp.	10 mL

Cream margarine and sugar in large bowl. Add eggs, 1 at a time, beating well after each addition. Add orange flavouring. Beat well.

Heat and stir chocolate and sour milk in heavy medium saucepan on medium-low until chocolate is melted. Mixture will look curdled. Remove from heat. Let stand for 5 minutes.

Combine flour, baking soda and salt in medium bowl. Add to margarine mixture in 3 additions, alternating with chocolate mixture in 2 additions, beginning and ending with flour mixture. Divide and spread evenly in 2 greased 8 inch (20 cm) round pans. Bake in 350°F (175°C) oven for about 25 minutes until wooden pick inserted in centre comes out clean. Let stand in pans for 5 minutes before inverting onto wire racks to cool completely.

Chocolate Orange Icing: Beat all 5 ingredients in medium bowl until smooth. Makes about 3 cups (750 mL) icing. Place 1 cake layer on serving plate. Spread with 3/4 cup (175 mL) icing. Place second layer on top. Spread top and side with remaining icing. Cuts into 12 wedges.

1 wedge: 538 Calories; 23.3 g Total Fat (11.2 g Mono, 1.8 g Poly, 9 g Sat); 59 mg Cholesterol; 80 g Carbohydrate; 2 g Fibre; 7 g Protein; 430 mg Sodium

Pictured on page 7.

A recipe this old and this good lasts through the years and stands the test of time. You can omit the topping and use as a shortcake.

Lazy Daisy Cake

Large eggs	2	2
Granulated sugar	1 cup	250 mL
Vanilla	1 tsp.	5 mL
All-purpose flour	1 cup	250 mL
Baking powder	1 tsp.	5 mL
Salt	1/2 tsp.	2 mL
Milk	1/2 cup	125 mL
Hard margarine (or butter)	1 tbsp.	15 mL
COCONUT TOPPING		
Hard margarine (or butter)	3 tbsp.	50 mL
Brown sugar, packed	1/2 cup	125 mL
Half-and-half cream (or milk)	2 tbsp.	30 mL
Flake coconut	1/2 cup	125 mL

Beat eggs in medium bowl until frothy. Add sugar, 2 tbsp. (30 mL) at a time while beating, until thickened. Add vanilla. Beat well.

Combine flour, baking powder and salt in small bowl. Add to egg mixture. Stir.

Heat and stir milk and margarine in small heavy saucepan on medium until margarine is melted. Add to flour mixture. Stir well. Spread batter evenly in greased 9 x 9 inch (22 x 22 cm) pan. Bake in 350°F (175°C) oven for 25 to 30 minutes until wooden pick inserted in centre comes out clean.

Coconut Topping: Measure margarine, brown sugar and cream into medium saucepan. Bring to a rolling boil on medium-high, stirring occasionally. Remove from heat.

Add coconut. Stir. Spread evenly over warm cake. Return to oven for about 3 minutes until top is bubbling. Let stand in pan on wire rack until cool. Cuts into 12 pieces.

1 piece: 226 Calories; 7.7 g Total Fat (3.1 g Mono, 0.6 g Poly, 3.6 g Sat); 37 mg Cholesterol; 37 g Carbohydrate; 1 g Fibre; 3 g Protein; 198 mg Sodium

Pictured on page 9.

Very pretty, moist cake with a tangy lime bite. Serve with Juicy Berries for an extra-special treat.

juicy berries

Combine 2 cups (500 mL) whole fresh berries (such as blackberries, blueberries or raspberries) and sliced strawberries in medium bowl. Add 1 cup (250 mL) white grape juice and 1/2 cup (125 mL) white corn syrup. Stir gently until coated. Chill for 1 hour to blend flavours. Serve with Lime Poppy Seed Cake.

juicy berries variation

Ice wine is a slightly more expensive, but delightful way to flavour berries. Omit white grape juice and corn syrup. Add 1/2 to 3/4 cup (125 to 175 mL) ice wine to 1 1/2 to 3 cups (375 to 750 mL) berries. Stir gently. A sweet dessert wine may be used instead of ice wine.

Lime Poppy Seed Cake

Milk	1 cup	250 mL
Poppy seeds	3 tbsp.	50 mL
Egg whites (large), room temperature	3	3
Almond flavouring	1 tsp.	5 mL
Hard margarine (or butter), softened	1 cup	250 mL
Granulated sugar	1 1/4 cups	300 mL
Egg yolks (large)	3	3
Finely grated lime zest	1 tbsp.	15 mL
All-purpose flour	2 cups	500 mL
Baking powder	1 tbsp.	15 mL
Salt	1/2 tsp.	2 mL
Hot water	2 tbsp.	30 mL
Icing (confectioner's) sugar	3/4 cup	175 mL
Lime juice	6 tbsp.	100 mL

Heat and stir milk and poppy seeds in small saucepan on medium until very hot, but not boiling. Remove from heat. Let stand until room temperature.

Beat egg whites and flavouring in medium bowl until stiff peaks form. Set aside.

Cream margarine and granulated sugar in large bowl. Add egg yolks, lime zest and milk mixture. Beat well.

Combine flour, baking powder and salt in small bowl. Add to margarine mixture. Beat well. Fold egg white mixture into flour mixture until no white streaks remain. Spread evenly in greased 10 inch (25 cm) angel food tube pan or 10 inch (25 cm) springform pan. Bake in 325°F (160°C) oven for about 1 hour until wooden pick inserted in centre of cake comes out clean. Let stand in pan for 10 minutes before removing to serving plate.

Stir hot water into icing sugar in small bowl until smooth. Add lime juice. Stir. Drizzle over hot cake, allowing syrup to soak in. Cool. Cuts into 12 wedges.

1 wedge: 384 Calories; 18.8 g Total Fat (11.2 g Mono, 2.6 g Poly, 4 g Sat); 55 mg Cholesterol; 50 g Carbohydrate; 1 g Fibre; 5 g Protein; 408 mg Sodium

Pictured on page 11.

Rich and delicious. Very moist. Freezes well.

Date Cake

Chopped pitted dates	1 1/2 cups	375 mL
Baking soda	1 1/2 tsp.	7 mL
Boiling water	1 1/2 cups	375 mL
Hard margarine (or butter), softened	3/4 cup	175 mL
Brown sugar, packed	1 cup	250 mL
Granulated sugar	1/2 cup	125 mL
Large eggs	2	2
Vanilla	1 tsp.	5 mL
All-purpose flour	2 1/2 cups	625 mL
Baking powder	1 1/2 tsp.	7 mL
Salt	1/2 tsp.	2 mL
Hard margarine (or butter)	1/3 cup	75 mL
Brown sugar, packed	1 cup	250 mL
Half-and-half cream (or milk)	3 tbsp.	50 mL
Fine coconut	1 cup	250 mL

Place dates in medium bowl. Sprinkle with baking soda. Pour boiling water over top. Set aside until cool. Stir.

Cream next 3 ingredients in large bowl. Add eggs, 1 at a time, beating well after each addition. Add vanilla. Beat.

Combine flour, baking powder and salt in small bowl. Add to margarine mixture in 3 additions, alternating with date mixture in 2 additions, beginning and ending with flour mixture. Spread evenly in greased 9 x 13 inch (22 x 33 cm) pan. Bake in 325°F (160°C) oven for 40 to 50 minutes until wooden pick inserted in centre comes out clean.

Measure next 3 ingredients into medium saucepan. Bring to a rolling boil on medium-high, stirring occasionally. Remove from heat.

Add coconut. Stir. Spread evenly over warm cake. Return to oven for about 3 minutes until top is bubbling. Let stand in pan on wire rack until cool. Cuts into 18 pieces.

1 piece: 365 Calories; 15.4 g Total Fat (7.7 g Mono, 1.3 g Poly, 5.5 g Sat); 24 mg Cholesterol; 56 g Carbohydrate; 2 g Fibre; 3 g Protein; 347 mg Sodium

Pictured on page 13.

A warm and comforting dessert on a chilly winter evening.

Sticky Ginger Fig Cake

Chopped figs	1 1/3 cups	325 mL
Baking soda	1 tsp.	5 mL
Boiling water	1 1/3 cups	325 mL
Hard margarine (or butter), softened	1/3 cup	75 mL
Brown sugar, packed	2/3 cup	150 mL
Large eggs	2	2
All-purpose flour	1 cup	250 mL
Baking powder	2 tsp.	10 mL
Minced crystallized ginger	1/4 cup	60 mL
CINNAMON BRANDY SAUCE		
Hard margarine (or butter), cut up	1/2 cup	125 mL
Brown sugar, packed	1/2 cup	125 mL
Whipping cream	1/2 cup	125 mL
Brandy	2 tbsp.	30 mL
Ground cinnamon	1/2 tsp.	2 mL

Place figs in medium bowl. Sprinkle with baking soda. Pour boiling water over top. Let stand for 10 minutes. Process (with liquid) in blender or food processor until almost smooth (see Safety Tip).

Cream margarine and brown sugar in large bowl. Add eggs, 1 at a time, beating well after each addition.

Combine flour, baking powder and ginger in small bowl. Add to margarine mixture. Stir well. Add fig mixture. Stir. Line bottom and side of greased 8 inch (20 cm) springform pan with parchment (not waxed) paper. Spread batter evenly in pan. Bake in 350°F (175°C) oven for about 50 minutes until wooden pick inserted in centre of cake comes out clean. Let stand in pan for 10 minutes before removing to wire rack to cool.

Cinnamon Brandy Sauce: Heat and stir all 5 ingredients in medium saucepan on medium until boiling. Boil for about 5 minutes, without stirring, until slightly thickened. Let stand for 5 minutes. Makes 1 cup (250 mL) sauce. Drizzle over individual servings of warm cake. Cuts into 8 wedges.

1 wedge: 545 Calories; 27 g Total Fat (15.2 g Mono, 2.6 g Poly, 7.8 g Sat); 72 mg Cholesterol; 73 g Carbohydrate; 4 g Fibre; 5 g Protein; 530 mg Sodium

Pictured on page 15.

Safety Tip: Follow blender manufacturer's instructions for processing hot liquids. If in doubt, we recommend using a hand blender.

Simple and delicious. Dust with icing sugar instead of the icing for a less sweet dessert.

White Chocolate Pound Cake

White chocolate baking squares (1 oz., 28 g, each), chopped	4	4
Evaporated milk	1 cup	250 mL
Hard margarine (or butter), softened	1 cup	250 mL
Granulated sugar	1 2/3 cups	400 mL
Large eggs	5	5
All-purpose flour	2 3/4 cups	675 mL
Baking soda	1/2 tsp.	2 mL
Salt	1/2 tsp.	2 mL
WHITE CHOCOLATE ICING		
Hard margarine (or butter)	1/4 cup	60 mL
White chocolate baking squares (1 oz., 28 g, each), chopped	3	3
Icing (confectioner's) sugar	2 cups	500 mL
Milk	1 tbsp.	15 mL
Vanilla	1/2 tsp.	2 mL

Heat and stir chocolate and evaporated milk in heavy medium saucepan on medium-low until chocolate is melted. Remove from heat. Let stand for 5 minutes.

Cream margarine and sugar in large bowl. Add eggs, 1 at a time, beating well after each addition.

Combine flour, baking soda and salt in medium bowl. Add to margarine mixture in 3 additions, alternating with chocolate mixture in 2 additions, beginning and ending with flour mixture. Spread evenly in greased 12 cup (3 L) bundt pan. Bake in 325°F (160°C) oven for about 1 hour until wooden pick inserted in centre of cake comes out clean. Let stand in pan for 20 minutes before inverting onto wire rack to cool completely.

White Chocolate Icing: Heat margarine and chocolate in small heavy saucepan on lowest heat, stirring often, until chocolate is almost melted. Do not overheat. Remove from heat. Stir until smooth.

Add icing sugar, milk and vanilla. Beat until smooth. Add more milk if necessary until barely pourable consistency. Drizzle over cake. Cuts into 16 wedges.

1 wedge: 467 Calories; 20.7 g Total Fat (11.7 g Mono, 1.9 g Poly, 5.8 g Sat); 71 mg Cholesterol; 65 g Carbohydrate; 1 g Fibre; 7 g Protein; 343 mg Sodium

Pictured on page 17.

A pretty contrast—amber pumpkin on dark gingersnap crust. Tastes as good as it looks. Make a day ahead. Freezes well.

Pumpkin Cheesecake

GINGERSNAP CRUMB CRUST		
Hard margarine (or butter)	1/4 cup	60 mL
Finely crushed gingersnap cookies	1 1/4 cups	300 mL
FILLING		
Blocks of cream cheese (8 oz., 250 g, each), softened	2	2
Granulated sugar	2/3 cup	150 mL
Large eggs	2	2
Can of pure pumpkin (no spices)	14 oz.	398 mL
Ground cinnamon	1/2 tsp.	2 mL
Ground nutmeg	1/2 tsp.	2 mL
Ground ginger	1/2 tsp.	2 mL
Salt	1/2 tsp.	2 mL

Gingersnap Crumb Crust: Melt margarine in medium saucepan. Remove from heat. Add crushed gingersnaps. Stir well. Press firmly in ungreased 9 inch (22 cm) springform pan. Bake in 350°F (175°C) oven for 10 minutes. Let stand until cool.

Filling: Beat cream cheese and sugar in large bowl until smooth. Add eggs, 1 at a time, beating after each addition until just combined.

Add remaining 5 ingredients. Beat well. Spread evenly over crust. Bake for 50 to 60 minutes until centre is almost set. Run knife around inside edge of pan to allow cheesecake to settle evenly. Let stand in pan on wire rack until cooled completely. Chill overnight. Cuts into 12 wedges.

1 wedge: 302 Calories; 20.7 g Total Fat (7.8 g Mono, 1.2 g Poly, 10.5 g Sat); 82 mg Cholesterol; 25 g Carbohydrate; 1 g Fibre; 5 g Protein; 360 mg Sodium

Pictured on page 19.

Garnish with whipped topping and whole cookies for an extra-special look that's sure to make the kids smile.

Cookie Cheesecake

COOKIE CRUMB CRUST

Hard margarine (or butter)	2 tbsp.	30 mL
Finely crushed cream-filled chocolate cookies	1 1/2 cups	375 mL

FILLING

Blocks of light cream cheese (8 oz., 250 g, each), softened	3	3
Granulated sugar	1 cup	250 mL
Vanilla	1 1/2 tsp.	7 mL
Whipping cream	1 cup	250 mL
Large eggs	3	3
Coarsely chopped cream-filled chocolate cookies	1 cup	250 mL

Cookie Crumb Crust: Melt margarine in medium saucepan. Remove from heat. Add crushed cookies. Stir well. Press firmly in bottom and 1/2 inch (12 mm) up side of greased 10 inch (25 cm) springform pan.

Filling: Beat cream cheese, sugar and vanilla in large bowl until smooth. Add whipping cream. Beat. Add eggs, 1 at a time, beating after each addition until just combined.

Fold in chopped cookies until evenly distributed. Spread evenly over crust. Bake in 325°F (160°C) oven for about 1 1/4 hours until centre is almost set. Run knife around inside edge of pan to allow cheesecake to settle evenly. Let stand in pan on wire rack until cooled completely. Chill overnight. Cuts into 16 wedges.

1 wedge: 318 Calories; 20.2 g Total Fat (7.7 g Mono, 1.2 g Poly, 9.7 g Sat); 88 mg Cholesterol; 28 g Carbohydrate; trace Fibre; 7 g Protein; 452 mg Sodium

Pictured on page 21.

Mint and chocolate make a refreshing after-dinner dessert. Made using a microwave oven. Serve with a hot cup of coffee or a cool glass of milk.

Crème de Menthe Cheesecake

CHOCOLATE CRUMB CRUST		
Hard margarine (or butter)	1/4 cup	60 mL
Chocolate wafer crumbs	1 1/4 cups	300 mL
Granulated sugar (optional)	2 tbsp.	30 mL
FILLING		
Blocks of cream cheese (4 oz., 125 g, each), softened	3	3
Granulated sugar	1/2 cup	125 mL
Large eggs	2	2
Mint-flavoured liqueur (such as green Crème de Menthe)	1/3 cup	75 mL
CHOCOLATE SOUR CREAM TOPPING		
Semi-sweet chocolate chips	1/2 cup	125 mL
Sour cream	1/2 cup	125 mL

Chocolate Crumb Crust: Place margarine in microwave-safe medium bowl. Microwave, uncovered, on high (100%) for about 35 seconds until melted. Add wafer crumbs and sugar. Stir well. Press firmly in bottom and up side of 9 inch (22 cm) microwave-safe pie plate. Microwave, uncovered, on high (100%) for 2 minutes. Set aside.

Filling: Beat cream cheese and sugar in large bowl until smooth. Add eggs, 1 at a time, beating after each addition until just combined. Add liqueur. Beat well. Spread evenly in crust. Cover with waxed paper. Microwave on medium (50%) for about 10 minutes, turning dish halfway through baking time if microwave doesn't have turntable, until centre is set. Let stand for 5 minutes.

Chocolate Sour Cream Topping: Place chips in 1 cup (250 mL) liquid measure. Microwave, uncovered, on medium (50%) for about 2 minutes until almost melted. Do not overheat. Stir until smooth. Add sour cream. Stir well. Spread evenly over filling. Chill for 3 to 4 hours until set. Cuts into 8 wedges.

1 wedge: 486 Calories; 31.6 g Total Fat (12.1 g Mono, 1.9 g Poly, 15.8 g Sat); 111 mg Cholesterol; 41 g Carbohydrate; 1 g Fibre; 7 g Protein; 340 mg Sodium

Pictured on page 23.

An attractive, rosy-coloured dessert. Cream cheese and cherries are always a favourite.

Cherry Chilled Cheesecake

GRAHAM CRUMB CRUST

Hard margarine (or butter)	1/3 cup	75 mL
Graham cracker crumbs	1 1/4 cups	300 mL
Brown sugar, packed	2 tbsp.	30 mL

FILLING

Block of cream cheese, softened	8 oz.	250 g
Icing (confectioner's) sugar	1 1/2 cups	375 mL
Vanilla	1/2 tsp.	2 mL
Can of cherry pie filling	19 oz.	540 mL
Frozen whipped topping, thawed (or whipped cream)	2 cups	500 mL

Graham Crumb Crust: Melt margarine in medium saucepan. Remove from heat. Add graham crumbs and brown sugar. Stir well. Reserve 3 tbsp. (50 mL) crumb mixture in small cup. Press remaining mixture firmly in ungreased 9 x 9 inch (22 x 22 cm) pan. Bake in 350°F (175°C) oven for 10 minutes. Let stand in pan on wire rack until cooled completely.

Filling: Beat cream cheese, icing sugar and vanilla in medium bowl until smooth. Add pie filling. Stir well. Spread evenly over crust.

Spread whipped topping evenly over filling. Sprinkle reserved crumb mixture over top. Chill overnight. Cuts into 12 pieces.

1 piece: 329 Calories; 17 g Total Fat (6.2 g Mono, 1 g Poly, 8.8 g Sat); 23 mg Cholesterol; 43 g Carbohydrate; 1 g Fibre; 3 g Protein; 189 mg Sodium

Pictured on page 27.

Mini-Chip Cheesecakes

Chocolate wafers	12	12
Blocks of light cream cheese (8 oz., 250 g, each), softened	2	2
Granulated sugar	3/4 cup	175 mL
Large eggs	2	2
Vanilla	1 tsp.	5 mL
Mini semi-sweet chocolate chips	1/2 cup	125 mL
Mini semi-sweet chocolate chips	1/2 cup	125 mL

This make-ahead dessert is a favourite with young and old. Garnish with whipped topping and chocolate curls.

Line 12 ungreased muffin cups with large paper liners. Place 1 wafer in bottom of each liner.

Beat cream cheese and sugar in medium bowl until smooth. Add eggs, 1 at a time, beating after each addition until just combined. Add vanilla. Beat.

Heat first amount of chips in small heavy saucepan on lowest heat, stirring often, until chocolate is almost melted. Do not overheat. Remove from heat. Stir until smooth. Add to cream cheese mixture. Stir.

Fold second amount of chips into cream cheese mixture until evenly distributed. Divide and spoon over wafers. Bake in 325°F (160°C) oven for 25 to 30 minutes until set. Let stand in pan on wire rack until cool. Chill for 2 to 3 hours. Makes 12 mini-cheesecakes.

1 mini-cheesecake: 255 Calories; 14.2 g Total Fat (4.8 g Mono, 0.6 g Poly, 7.8 g Sat); 62 mg Cholesterol; 29 g Carbohydrate; 1 g Fibre; 6 g Protein; 338 mg Sodium

Pictured on page 27.

This treat has a built-in topping—no icing required.

Cheesy Cupcakes

Block of light cream cheese, softened	8 oz.	250 g
Granulated sugar	1/2 cup	125 mL
Large egg	1	1
Semi-sweet chocolate chips	1 cup	250 mL
All-purpose flour	1 1/2 cups	375 mL
Granulated sugar	1 cup	250 mL
Cocoa, sifted if lumpy	1/3 cup	75 mL
Baking soda	1 tsp.	5 mL
Salt	1/2 tsp.	2 mL
Hard margarine (or butter), softened	6 tbsp.	100 mL
Warm water	1 cup	250 mL
Vanilla	1 tsp.	5 mL

Beat cream cheese, first amount of sugar and egg in small bowl until smooth. Add chips. Stir. Set aside.

Combine next 5 ingredients in large bowl. Make a well in centre.

Add margarine, warm water and vanilla to well. Beat for about 2 minutes until smooth. Line 20 ungreased muffin cups with large paper liners. Divide and spoon batter into each cup. Divide and spoon cream cheese mixture over batter. Bake in 350°F (175°C) oven for 30 to 35 minutes until wooden pick inserted in centre of cupcake comes out clean. Makes 20 cupcakes.

1 cupcake: 207 Calories; 9.1 g Total Fat (4.1 g Mono, 0.6 g Poly, 3.9 g Sat); 19 mg Cholesterol; 30 g Carbohydrate; 1 g Fibre; 3 g Protein; 256 mg Sodium

Pictured on page 27.

Top Right: Cheesy Cupcakes, above
Centre Left: Mini-Chip Cheesecakes, page 25
Bottom Right: Cherry Chilled Cheesecake, page 24

A wonderful blend of flavours in a sweet, chewy macaroon! Almost too pretty to eat—but not quite!

note

To toast nuts, place in single layer in ungreased shallow pan. Bake in 350°F (175°C) oven for 5 to 8 minutes, stirring or shaking often, until desired doneness.

Cherry Coconut Macaroons

Flake coconut	2 cups	500 mL
Maraschino cherries, blotted dry and chopped	3/4 cup	175 mL
Sliced almonds, toasted (see Note)	1/2 cup	125 mL
All-purpose flour	1/2 cup	125 mL
Salt	1/4 tsp.	1 mL
Egg whites (large)	4	4
Almond flavouring	1/2 tsp.	2 mL
Granulated sugar	1/2 cup	125 mL

Combine first 5 ingredients in medium bowl.

Beat egg whites and flavouring on medium in large bowl until frothy. Add sugar, 1 tbsp. (15 mL) at a time while beating, until soft peaks form. Fold coconut mixture into egg white mixture until just moistened. Drop, using 2 tbsp. (30 mL) for each, about 2 inches (5 cm) apart, onto greased cookie sheets. Bake in 325°F (160°C) oven for about 15 minutes until edges are golden. Let stand on cookie sheets for 5 minutes before removing to wire racks to cool. Makes about 2 1/2 dozen (30) macaroons.

1 macaroon: 85 Calories; 5.1 g Total Fat (0.8 g Mono, 0.3 g Poly, 3.7 g Sat); 0 mg Cholesterol; 9 g Carbohydrate; 1 g Fibre; 2 g Protein; 30 mg Sodium

Pictured on page 29.

Top Right: Cherry Coconut Macaroons, above
Centre Left: Cranberry Chip Cookies, page 30
Bottom: Pecan Caramel Kisses, page 31

Festive, flavourful cookies that will satisfy any sweet craving!

Cranberry Chip Cookies

Large eggs	2	2
Brown sugar, packed	1 2/3 cups	400 mL
Vanilla	1 tsp.	5 mL
All-purpose flour	1 3/4 cups	425 mL
Baking powder	1 tsp.	5 mL
Baking soda	1/2 tsp.	2 mL
Cooking oil	1/2 cup	125 mL
Dried cranberries	1/2 cup	125 mL
Unsalted peanuts	1/2 cup	125 mL
White chocolate chips	1/2 cup	125 mL

Beat eggs, brown sugar and vanilla in large bowl until light and creamy.

Combine flour, baking powder and soda in small bowl. Add to egg mixture. Stir well.

Add remaining 4 ingredients. Stir until evenly distributed. Cover. Chill for 1 hour. Roll dough into balls, using 1 tbsp. (15 mL) for each. Arrange balls, about 2 inches (5 cm) apart, on greased cookie sheets. Bake in 350°F (175°C) oven for about 15 minutes until golden. Let stand on cookie sheets for 5 minutes before removing to wire racks to cool. Makes about 3 1/2 dozen (42) cookies.

1 cookie: 107 Calories; 4.6 g Total Fat (2.4 g Mono, 1.2 g Poly, 0.8 g Sat); 11 mg Cholesterol; 16 g Carbohydrate; 1 g Fibre; 1 g Protein; 33 mg Sodium

Pictured on page 29.

Pecan Caramel Kisses

Egg whites (large), room temperature	2	2
Cream of tartar	1/8 tsp.	0.5 mL
Maple flavouring	1/4 tsp.	1 mL
Icing (confectioner's) sugar	1 cup	250 mL
Chopped pecans, toasted (see Note)	1/3 cup	75 mL
Caramels	10	10
Milk	2 tsp.	10 mL

Beat egg whites, cream of tartar and flavouring in medium bowl until stiff peaks form. Add icing sugar, 2 tbsp. (30 mL) at a time while beating, until very glossy and stiff.

Fold pecans into egg white mixture until evenly distributed. Drop, using 1 tbsp. (15 mL) for each, about 2 inches (5 cm) apart, onto greased parchment (not waxed) paper-lined cookie sheets. Bake in 275°F (140°C) oven for about 30 minutes until dry and edges are golden. Let stand on cookie sheets for 5 minutes before removing to wire racks to cool.

Heat and stir caramels and milk in small saucepan on medium-low until smooth. Remove from heat. Let stand for 5 minutes. Drizzle over meringues. Makes about 2 1/2 dozen (30) meringues.

1 meringue: 37 Calories; 1.2 g Total Fat (0.6 g Mono, 0.2 g Poly, 0.3 g Sat); 0 mg Cholesterol; 7 g Carbohydrate; trace Fibre; 0 g Protein; 10 mg Sodium

Pictured on page 29.

Light and crispy meringues drizzled with sticky caramel sauce. Crunchy toasted pecans make this an immensely satisfying sweet treat.

note

To toast nuts, place in single layer in ungreased shallow pan. Bake in 350°F (175°C) oven for 5 to 8 minutes, stirring or shaking often, until desired doneness.

variation

For smaller cookies, roll dough into 1 1/2 inch (3.8 cm) balls. Arrange balls, about 2 inches (5 cm) apart, on greased cookie sheets. Flatten cookies slightly with flat-bottomed glass dipped in second amount of granulated sugar. Bake in 375°F (190°C) oven for 8 to 10 minutes until golden. Let stand on cookie sheets for 5 minutes before removing to wire racks to cool. Makes about 5 dozen (60) cookies.

Giant Candy Bar Cookies

Hard margarine (or butter), softened	1 cup	250 mL
Granulated sugar	1 cup	250 mL
Brown sugar, packed	1 cup	250 mL
Large eggs	2	2
Vanilla	2 tsp.	10 mL
All-purpose flour	2 cups	500 mL
Baking powder	1 tsp.	5 mL
Baking soda	1 tsp.	5 mL
Salt	1/2 tsp.	2 mL
Quick-cooking rolled oats (not instant)	2 1/3 cups	575 mL
Chocolate-covered crispy toffee bars (such as Skor or Heath), 1 1/2 oz. (39 g) each, chopped	8	8
Granulated sugar	1/4 cup	60 mL

Cream margarine, first amount of granulated sugar and brown sugar in large bowl. Add eggs, 1 at a time, beating well after each addition. Add vanilla. Beat.

Combine next 4 ingredients in small bowl. Add to margarine mixture. Stir until just moistened.

Add rolled oats and chocolate bar pieces. Stir well. Roll into 2 inch (5 cm) balls. Arrange 4 to 6 balls, about 4 inches (10 cm) apart, on greased cookie sheet.

Dip flat-bottomed glass into second amount of granulated sugar. Flatten cookies to 1/2 inch (12 mm) thickness, dipping glass in sugar as necessary. Bake in 375°F (190°C) oven for about 11 minutes until golden. Let stand on cookie sheet for 5 minutes before removing to wire rack to cool. Repeat with remaining dough. Makes about 3 dozen (36) cookies.

1 cookie: 204 Calories; 9.2 g Total Fat (3.8 g Mono, 0.8 g Poly, 1.3 g Sat); 17 mg Cholesterol; 29 g Carbohydrate; 1 g Fibre; 3 g Protein; 168 mg Sodium

Pictured on page 33.

Also known as Swedish Pastry and Thumbprints. So good, you'll need to make more!

Swedish Tea Cakes

Hard margarine (or butter), softened	1/2 cup	125 mL
Brown sugar, packed	1/4 cup	60 mL
Egg yolk (large)	1	1
All-purpose flour	1 cup	250 mL
Baking powder	1/2 tsp.	2 mL
Salt	1/8 tsp.	0.5 mL
Egg white (large), fork-beaten	1	1
Finely chopped nuts (your favourite), for coating	2/3 cup	150 mL
Jam or jelly (red is best), your favourite	6 tbsp.	100 mL

Cream margarine and brown sugar in large bowl. Add egg yolk. Beat well.

Combine flour, baking powder and salt in small bowl. Add to margarine mixture. Stir until stiff dough forms. Roll dough into balls, using 2 tsp. (10 mL) for each.

Dip balls into egg white. Roll in nuts. Arrange balls, about 2 inches (5 cm) apart, on greased cookie sheets. Dent each with thumb. Bake in 325°F (160°C) oven for 5 minutes. Remove from oven. Press dents again. Bake for 10 to 15 minutes until golden. Let stand on cookie sheets for 5 minutes before removing to wire racks.

Fill each dent with 1 tsp. (5 mL) jam. (Unfilled tea cakes may be stored in airtight container and filled with jam just before serving.) Makes about 20 tea cakes.

1 tea cake: 125 Calories; 7.7 g Total Fat (3.8 g Mono, 2.2 g Poly, 1.2 g Sat); 11 mg Cholesterol; 13 g Carbohydrate; 1 g Fibre; 2 g Protein; 88 mg Sodium

Pictured on page 35.

These are definitely more impressive than regular cookies but still easy enough for kids to make! A tasty one-bite snack that will make you popular with kids and grown-ups alike.

cookie pizza

Press 3 cups (750 mL) cookie dough evenly in greased 12 inch (30 cm) pizza pan. Sprinkle with semi-sweet chocolate chips, butterscotch chips, candy-coated chocolate candies (such as Smarties or M & M's), cereal flakes, coconut, peanuts or any other favourites. Bake in 375°F (190°C) oven for 12 to 15 minutes until puffy and golden. Serve warm or cold. Cuts into 16 wedges.

Peanut Butter Hide-Aways

Hard margarine (or butter), softened	1/2 cup	125 mL
Smooth peanut butter	1/2 cup	125 mL
Granulated sugar	1/3 cup	75 mL
Brown sugar, packed	1/3 cup	75 mL
Large egg	1	1
All-purpose flour	1 1/3 cups	325 mL
Baking powder	1 tsp.	5 mL
Baking soda	1/2 tsp.	2 mL
Salt	1/4 tsp.	1 mL
Miniature peanut butter cups	36	36

Beat first 4 ingredients in large bowl until light and creamy. Add egg. Beat well.

Combine next 4 ingredients in small bowl. Add to margarine mixture. Stir until just moistened. Dough will be stiff. Roll into 36 balls, using 1 tbsp. (15 mL) for each. Place 1 ball in each of 36 ungreased mini-muffin cups. Bake in 375°F (190°C) oven for about 10 minutes until puffy and golden. Remove from oven.

Remove and discard foil cup from peanut butter cups. Press 1 peanut butter cup into each hot cookie. Loosen edges of cookies with tip of knife. Chill for 20 minutes before removing from pan. If cookies are difficult to remove, tap bottom of pan several times on hard surface or let stand until cookies are room temperature. Makes 3 dozen (36) cookies.

1 cookie: 120 Calories; 7.3 g Total Fat (3.5 g Mono, 1.1 g Poly, 2.1 g Sat); 7 mg Cholesterol; 12 g Carbohydrate; 1 g Fibre; 3 g Protein; 119 mg Sodium

Pictured on page 39.

Oatmeal Chip Cookies

Hard margarine (or butter), softened	1 cup	250 mL
Brown sugar, packed	2 cups	500 mL
Large eggs	2	2
Vanilla	1 tsp.	5 mL
All-purpose flour	2 cups	500 mL
Baking powder	1 tsp.	5 mL
Baking soda	1/2 tsp.	2 mL
Quick-cooking rolled oats (not instant)	2 cups	500 mL
Semi-sweet chocolate chips	2 cups	500 mL
Medium unsweetened coconut	3/4 cup	175 mL

Beat margarine and sugar in large bowl until light and creamy. Add eggs, 1 at a time, beating well after each addition. Add vanilla. Beat.

Combine flour, baking powder and soda in small bowl. Add to margarine mixture. Stir well.

Add remaining 3 ingredients. Stir until well distributed. Drop, using 2 tbsp. (30 mL) for each, about 2 inches (5 cm) apart, onto greased cookie sheets. Bake in 350°F (175°C) oven for 8 to 10 minutes until golden. Let stand on cookie sheets for 5 minutes before removing to wire racks to cool. Makes about 5 dozen (60) cookies.

1 cookie: *126 Calories; 6.2 g Total Fat (2.9 g Mono, 0.5 g Poly, 2.5 g Sat); 7 mg Cholesterol; 17 g Carbohydrate; 1 g Fibre; 2 g Protein; 61 mg Sodium*

Pictured below.

Chocolate and oatmeal make the ultimate cookie. A great favourite.

oatmeal chip pizza

Press 3 cups (750 mL) cookie dough evenly in greased 12 inch (30 cm) pizza pan. Sprinkle with semi-sweet chocolate chips, butterscotch chips, candy-coated chocolate candies (such as Smarties or M & M's), cereal flakes, coconut, peanuts or any other favourites. Bake in 350°F (175°C) oven for 12 to 15 minutes until golden. Cuts into 16 wedges.

These delicious cookies contain no flour. Soft and chewy. Makes a huge batch. Use an extra-large bowl, plastic tub or roaster to mix these.

rainbow chip pizza

Press 3 cups (750 mL) cookie dough evenly in greased 12 inch (30 cm) pizza pan. Sprinkle with semi-sweet chocolate chips, butterscotch chips, candy-coated chocolate candies (such as Smarties or M & M's), cereal flakes, coconut, peanuts or any other favourites. Bake in 350°F (175°C) oven for 12 to 15 minutes until golden. Cuts into 16 wedges.

Rainbow Chip Cookies

Smooth peanut butter	6 cups	1.5 L
Brown sugar, packed	6 cups	1.5 L
Granulated sugar	4 cups	1 L
Hard margarine (or butter), softened	2 cups	500 mL
Large eggs	12	12
Vanilla	1 tbsp.	15 mL
Golden corn syrup	1 tbsp.	15 mL
Quick-cooking rolled oats (not instant)	18 cups	4.5 L
Semi-sweet chocolate chips	2 cups	500 mL
Candy-coated chocolate candies (such as Smarties or M & M's)	2 cups	500 mL
Baking soda	8 tsp.	40 mL

Beat first 4 ingredients in extra-large bowl until light and creamy. Add eggs, 2 at a time, beating well after each addition. Add vanilla and corn syrup. Beat.

Add remaining 4 ingredients. Stir well. Roll into balls, using 2 tbsp. (30 mL) for each. Arrange balls, about 2 inches (5 cm) apart, on greased cookie sheets. Flatten slightly. Bake in 350°F (175°C) oven for 7 to 8 minutes until golden. Overbaking will make them hard. Let stand on cookie sheets for 5 minutes before removing to wire racks to cool. Makes about 26 dozen (312) cookies.

1 cookie: 108 Calories; 5.2 g Total Fat (2.4 g Mono, 1 g Poly, 1.1 g Sat); 8 mg Cholesterol; 14 g Carbohydrate; 1 g Fibre; 3 g Protein; 78 mg Sodium

Pictured on page 39.

Top Left: Rainbow Chip Cookies, above
Bottom Right: Peanut Butter Hide-Aways, page 36

Pretty, 3-layered cookie. Freezes well before, or after, baking.

Icebox Ribbons

Hard margarine (or butter), softened	1 cup	250 mL
Granulated sugar	1 cup	250 mL
Large egg	1	1
Vanilla	1 tsp.	5 mL
All-purpose flour	2 1/2 cups	625 mL
Baking powder	1 tsp.	5 mL
Salt	1/4 tsp.	1 mL
Red liquid (or paste) food colouring		
Chopped red glazed cherries	1/4 cup	60 mL
Medium unsweetened coconut	1/3 cup	75 mL
Semi-sweet chocolate chips	1/3 cup	75 mL
Chopped nuts (your favourite)	1/3 cup	75 mL

Cream margarine and sugar in large bowl. Add egg and vanilla. Beat well.

Combine flour, baking powder and salt in medium bowl. Add to margarine mixture. Stir until stiff dough forms. Divide dough into 3 equal portions.

Knead enough red food colouring into 1 portion of dough until pink. Add cherries. Knead until evenly distributed. Press in foil-lined 8 x 4 x 3 inch (20 x 10 x 7.5 cm) loaf pan.

Add coconut to second portion of dough. Knead until evenly distributed. Press evenly over pink layer.

Heat chips in small heavy saucepan on lowest heat, stirring often, until almost melted. Do not overheat. Remove from heat. Stir until smooth. Add chocolate and nuts to third portion of dough. Knead until no streaks remain. Press evenly over coconut layer. Cover with plastic wrap. Chill overnight. Remove from pan. Remove and discard foil. Cut into 1/4 inch (6 mm) thick slices. Cut each slice into 3 pieces. Arrange slices, about 2 inches (5 cm) apart, on greased cookie sheets. Bake in 350ºF (175ºC) oven for 10 to 12 minutes until edges are golden. Let stand on cookie sheets for 5 minutes before removing to wire racks to cool. Makes about 5 1/2 dozen (66) cookies.

1 cookie: 72 Calories; 4 g Total Fat (2.1 g Mono, 0.6 g Poly, 1.1 g Sat); 3 mg Cholesterol; 8 g Carbohydrate; trace Fibre; 1 g Protein; 50 mg Sodium

Pictured on page 43.

Noodle Power

Semi-sweet chocolate chips	1 cup	250 mL
Butterscotch chips	1 cup	250 mL
Hard margarine (or butter)	1/4 cup	60 mL
Smooth peanut butter	1/4 cup	60 mL
Dry chow mein noodles	2 cups	500 mL
Unsalted peanuts	1 cup	250 mL

These little stacks are shiny and ever so good. They are softer to bite into than other similar cookies.

Heat first 4 ingredients in large heavy saucepan on lowest heat, stirring often, until chips are almost melted. Do not overheat. Remove from heat. Stir until smooth.

Add noodles and peanuts. Stir until coated. Mixture will be soft. Drop, using 2 tsp. (10 mL) for each, onto waxed paper-lined cookie sheets. Let stand until set. May be chilled to hasten setting. Makes 2 1/2 dozen (30) cookies.

1 cookie: 123 Calories; 8.3 g Total Fat (3.7 g Mono, 1.9 g Poly, 2.2 g Sat); 0 mg Cholesterol; 12 g Carbohydrate; 1 g Fibre; 2 g Protein; 47 mg Sodium

Pictured on page 42.

Coconut Peaks

Flake coconut	3 cups	750 mL
Icing (confectioner's) sugar	2 cups	500 mL
Hard margarine (or butter), melted	1/4 cup	60 mL
Half-and-half cream (or milk)	2 tbsp.	30 mL
Semi-sweet chocolate chips	1 cup	250 mL
Hard margarine (or butter)	1 tbsp.	15 mL

These will take the spotlight on any plate of cookies! A no-bake treat that freezes well.

Combine first 4 ingredients in large bowl. Roll into balls, using 1/2 tbsp. (7 mL) for each. Squeeze tops to form peaks that resemble haystacks. Arrange on waxed paper-lined cookie sheet. Chill, uncovered, overnight.

Heat chips and second amount of margarine in small heavy saucepan on lowest heat, stirring often, until chips are almost melted. Do not overheat. Remove from heat. Stir until smooth. Dip peaks of cookies into chocolate mixture. Let stand until chocolate is set. Makes 2 1/2 dozen (30) cookies.

1 cookie: 143 Calories; 10 g Total Fat (2.2 g Mono, 0.3 g Poly, 7 g Sat); 0 mg Cholesterol; 15 g Carbohydrate; 1 g Fibre; 1 g Protein; 28 mg Sodium

Pictured on page 42.

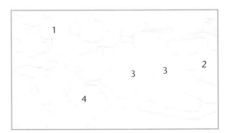

Photo Legend next page
1. Noodle Power, this page
2. Coconut Rum Diagonals, page 44
3. Icebox Ribbons, page 40
4. Coconut Peaks, this page

Pretty diamond-shaped cookies with an awesome flavour combination.

coconut diagonals

Omit the rum flavouring. Use same amount of vanilla.

Coconut Rum Diagonals

Hard margarine (or butter), softened	1/2 cup	125 mL
Granulated sugar	1/4 cup	60 mL
Vanilla	1 tsp.	5 mL
Salt	1/8 tsp.	0.5 mL
All-purpose flour	1 cup	250 mL
Flake coconut	1 cup	250 mL
Baking powder	1/2 tsp.	2 mL
RUM ICING		
Icing (confectioner's) sugar	1 cup	250 mL
Water	1 1/2 tbsp.	25 mL
Rum flavouring	1/2 tsp.	2 mL

Beat first 4 ingredients in large bowl until light and creamy.

Combine flour, coconut and baking powder in small bowl. Add to margarine mixture. Stir well. Divide dough into 6 equal portions. Roll each portion into 9 inch (22 cm) rope. Arrange ropes, about 2 inches (5 cm) apart, on greased cookie sheets. Bake in 350°F (175°C) oven for 18 to 22 minutes until golden. Let stand on cookie sheets on wire racks for 5 minutes.

Rum Icing: Stir all 3 ingredients in small bowl, adding more water or icing sugar if necessary until spreading consistency. Ice ropes while still warm. Cut each rope into 1 inch (2.5 cm) diagonals, for a total of 4 1/2 dozen (54) cookies.

1 diagonal: 50 Calories; 3 g Total Fat (1.2 g Mono, 0.2 g Poly, 1.4 g Sat); 0 mg Cholesterol; 6 g Carbohydrate; trace Fibre; 0 g Protein; 31 mg Sodium

Pictured on page 43.

These melt in your mouth! Garnish with your favourite Christmas candy.

Whipped Shortbread

Butter (not margarine), softened	1 cup	250 mL
Granulated sugar	1/2 cup	125 mL
All-purpose flour	1 1/2 cups	375 mL
Cornstarch	1/4 cup	60 mL

Beat butter and sugar in medium bowl until light and creamy.

(continued on next page)

Combine flour and cornstarch in small bowl. Add to butter mixture, 2 tbsp. (30 mL) at a time while beating, until smooth. Pipe 1 1/2 inch (3.8 cm) rosettes, about 2 inches (5 cm) apart, onto ungreased cookie sheets. Bake in 375°F (190°C) oven for 12 to 14 minutes until just golden. Let stand on cookie sheets for 5 minutes before removing to wire racks to cool. Makes 2 1/2 dozen (30) cookies.

1 cookie: 99 Calories; 6.6 g Total Fat (1.9 g Mono, 0.3 g Poly, 4.1 g Sat); 18 mg Cholesterol; 10 g Carbohydrate; trace Fibre; 1 g Protein; 66 mg Sodium

Pictured on page 47.

Candy Cane Cookies

Hard margarine (or butter), softened	1 cup	250 mL
Icing (confectioner's) sugar	1 cup	250 mL
Large egg	1	1
Almond flavouring	1 tsp.	5 mL
Vanilla	1 tsp.	5 mL
Peppermint flavouring	1/4 tsp.	1 mL
All-purpose flour	2 1/2 cups	625 mL
Baking powder	1 tsp.	5 mL
Salt	1 tsp.	5 mL
Red liquid food colouring	1/2 tsp.	2 mL

A fun cookie for the whole family to make together.

Beat first 6 ingredients in large bowl until light and creamy.

Combine flour, baking powder and salt in medium bowl. Add to margarine mixture. Stir until stiff dough forms. Divide dough into 2 equal portions.

Knead food colouring into 1 portion of dough until evenly tinted. Roll about 1 tsp. (5 mL) of each colour dough into 5 1/2 inch (14 cm) rope. Lay side by side. Pinch ends together. Twist and form into candy cane shape. Repeat with remaining dough. Arrange, about 2 inches (5 cm) apart, on greased cookie sheets. Bake in 350°F (175°C) oven for about 10 minutes until just golden. Let stand on cookie sheets for 5 minutes before removing to wire racks to cool. Makes about 4 1/2 dozen (54) cookies.

1 cookie: 65 Calories; 3.7 g Total Fat (2.4 g Mono, 0.4 g Poly, 0.8 g Sat); 4 mg Cholesterol; 7 g Carbohydrate; trace Fibre; 1 g Protein; 94 mg Sodium

Pictured on page 47.

These freeze well—a great way to get a head start on your holiday baking.

Sugar Cookies

Hard margarine (or butter), softened	3/4 cup	175 mL
Granulated sugar	3/4 cup	175 mL
Large egg	1	1
Vanilla	1 tsp.	5 mL
All-purpose flour	2 cups	500 mL
Baking soda	1 tsp.	5 mL
Cream of tartar	1 tsp.	5 mL
Ground cardamom (optional)	1/4 tsp.	1 mL
Salt	1/4 tsp.	1 mL

Cream margarine and sugar in large bowl. Add egg and vanilla. Beat well.

Combine remaining 5 ingredients in medium bowl. Add to margarine mixture. Stir until stiff dough forms. Roll dough out to 1/8 inch (3 mm) thickness on lightly floured surface. Cut out dough using lightly floured cookie cutters. Arrange cookies, about 2 inches (5 cm) apart, on greased cookie sheets. Bake in 350°F (175°C) oven for about 10 minutes until golden. Let stand on cookie sheets for 5 minutes before removing to wire racks to cool. Makes 7 dozen (84) cookies.

1 cookie: 35 Calories; 1.8 g Total Fat (1.2 g Mono, 0.2 g Poly, 0.4 g Sat); 3 mg Cholesterol; 4 g Carbohydrate; trace Fibre; 0 g Protein; 43 mg Sodium

Pictured on page 47.

Easy Glaze

Water	2 tsp.	10 mL
Icing (confectioner's) sugar	1/2 cup	125 mL
Liquid (or paste) food colouring		

Stir water into icing sugar in small bowl, adding more water or icing sugar if necessary until spreading consistency. Add food colouring, 1 drop at a time, stirring well after each addition until desired colour is reached. Makes about 6 tbsp. (100 mL).

6 tbsp. (100 mL) glaze: 247 Calories; 0.1 g Total Fat (0 g Mono, 0 g Poly, 0 g Sat); 0 mg Cholesterol; 63 g Carbohydrate; 0 g Fibre; 0 g Protein; 1 mg Sodium

Pictured on page 47 (on Sugar Cookies).

Top Left: Candy Cane Cookies, page 45
Top Right: Whipped Shortbread, page 44
Bottom Left: Sugar Cookies, this page

Tell the kids they can have cookies for breakfast—they'll love it!

Nutri-Cookies

Hard margarine (or butter), softened	1/2 cup	125 mL
Smooth peanut butter	1/2 cup	125 mL
Liquid honey	1 cup	250 mL
Large eggs	2	2
Vanilla	1 tsp.	5 mL
Quick-cooking rolled oats (not instant)	3 cups	750 mL
All-purpose flour	1 1/2 cups	375 mL
Unsweetened medium coconut	1 cup	250 mL
Sultana raisins	1 cup	250 mL
Natural wheat bran	3/4 cup	175 mL
Shelled sunflower seeds	1/2 cup	125 mL
Chopped walnuts (or your favourite)	1/2 cup	125 mL
Baking soda	1 tsp.	5 mL
Salt	1 tsp.	5 mL

Cream margarine and peanut butter in large bowl. Add honey, eggs and vanilla. Beat well.

Add remaining 9 ingredients. Stir well. Roll dough into balls, using 1 tbsp. (15 mL) for each. Flatten slightly. Arrange cookies, about 2 inches (5 cm) apart, on ungreased cookie sheets. Bake in 375°F (190°C) oven for about 12 minutes until golden. Let stand on cookie sheets for 5 minutes before removing to wire racks to cool. Makes 8 dozen (96) cookies.

1 cookie: 74 Calories; 3.5 g Total Fat (1.3 g Mono, 0.9 g Poly, 1.1 g Sat); 4 mg Cholesterol; 10 g Carbohydrate; 1 g Fibre; 2 g Protein; 59 mg Sodium

Pictured on page 49.

Soft Molasses Drops

An old-time recipe. Moist and spicy.

All-purpose flour	3 1/2 cups	875 mL
Granulated sugar	3/4 cup	175 mL
Ground ginger	1 tsp.	5 mL
Ground cinnamon	1 tsp.	5 mL
Salt	1/2 tsp.	2 mL
Fancy (mild) molasses	3/4 cup	175 mL
Hard margarine (or butter), softened	3/4 cup	175 mL
Large egg	1	1
Baking soda	1 1/2 tsp.	7 mL
Hot prepared strong coffee (or hot milk)	1/2 cup	125 mL

Measure first 8 ingredients, in order given, into large bowl. Stir.

Stir baking soda into hot coffee. Add to flour mixture. Beat well. Drop, using 1 tbsp. (15 mL) for each, about 2 inches (5 cm) apart, onto greased cookie sheets. Bake in 375°F (190°C) oven for 10 to 12 minutes until dry but soft. Let stand on cookie sheets for 5 minutes before removing to wire racks to cool. Makes 5 dozen (60) cookies.

1 cookie: 73 Calories; 2.6 g Total Fat (1.6 g Mono, 0.3 g Poly, 0.5 g Sat); 4 mg Cholesterol; 12 g Carbohydrate; trace Fibre; 1 g Protein; 83 mg Sodium

Pictured below.

Left and Top Centre: Soft Molasses Drops, this page
Bottom Centre: Nutri-Cookies, page 48
Right: Hermits, page 50

*One of the best known—and best
loved—drop cookies! Our cookie jar
was always filled with these.*

Hermits

Hard margarine (or butter), softened	1 cup	250 mL
Brown sugar, packed	1 1/2 cups	375 mL
Large eggs	3	3
Vanilla	1 tsp.	5 mL
All-purpose flour	3 cups	750 mL
Sultana raisins	1 cup	250 mL
Chopped pitted dates	1 cup	250 mL
Chopped walnuts (or your favourite)	2/3 cup	150 mL
Baking powder	1 tsp.	5 mL
Baking soda	1 tsp.	5 mL
Ground cinnamon	1 tsp.	5 mL
Ground nutmeg	1/2 tsp.	2 mL
Salt	1/2 tsp.	2 mL
Ground allspice	1/4 tsp.	1 mL

Cream margarine and sugar in large bowl. Add eggs, 1 at a time, beating well
after each addition. Add vanilla. Beat.

Add remaining 10 ingredients. Stir until well distributed. Drop, using 1 tbsp.
(15 mL) for each, about 2 inches (5 cm) apart, onto greased cookie sheets.
Bake in 375°F (190°C) oven for 6 to 8 minutes until golden. Let stand on cookie
sheets for 5 minutes before removing to wire racks to cool. Makes 4 1/2 dozen
(54) cookies.

*1 cookie: 117 Calories; 4.9 g Total Fat (2.7 g Mono, 1 g Poly, 0.9 g Sat); 12 mg Cholesterol; 17 g Carbohydrate;
1 g Fibre; 2 g Protein; 101 mg Sodium*

Pictured on page 49.

Butterscotch Cookies

Smooth peanut butter	3 tbsp.	50 mL
Butterscotch chips	1 cup	250 mL
Cornflakes cereal	3 cups	750 mL
Chopped pecans (or walnuts)	1/2 cup	125 mL

These no-bake cookies are golden and crunchy. Sweet, with a mild peanut butter flavour!

Heat peanut butter and chips in large heavy saucepan on lowest heat, stirring often, until chips are almost melted. Do not overheat. Remove from heat. Stir until smooth.

Add cereal and pecans. Stir until coated. Drop, using 2 tbsp. (30 mL) for each, onto waxed paper-lined cookie sheets. Let stand until set. Makes about 2 1/2 dozen (30) cookies.

1 cookie: 53 Calories; 2.4 g Total Fat (1.3 g Mono, 0.6 g Poly, 0.3 g Sat); 0 mg Cholesterol; 8 g Carbohydrate; trace Fibre; 1 g Protein; 36 mg Sodium

Pictured below.

An Italian favourite. This dessert (boh-KOHN-nee DOHL-chay) has meringue layers smothered with chocolate, strawberries and cream.

strawberry meringue shortcake

Trace ten 4 inch (10 cm) circles as directed in recipe. Divide and spoon egg white mixture into circles. Spread evenly to edges, forming raised sides. Bake as directed for about 30 minutes. To serve, fill with sweetened strawberries and top with whipped cream.

Bocconne Dolce

MERINGUE

Egg whites (large), room temperature	6	6
Cream of tartar	1/4 tsp.	1 mL
Granulated sugar	1 1/2 cups	375 mL

FILLING

Semi-sweet chocolate chips	1 cup	250 mL
Water	3 tbsp.	50 mL
Whipping cream	3 cups	750 mL
Granulated sugar	1/3 cup	75 mL
Vanilla	2 tsp.	10 mL
Fresh strawberries, sliced lengthwise	3 cups	750 mL

Fresh whole strawberries, for garnish
Chocolate curls (see Note, page 57),
   for garnish

Meringue: Beat egg whites and cream of tartar in medium bowl until soft peaks form. Add sugar, 1 tbsp. (15 mL) at a time while beating, until stiff peaks form and sugar is dissolved. Line bottoms of 2 baking sheets with parchment (not waxed) paper. Trace two 8 inch (20 cm) circles about 1 1/2 inches (3.8 cm) apart on first paper, and one 8 inch (20 cm) circle on second paper. Turn papers over (or use foil with circles marked on top). Divide and spoon meringue onto circles. Spread evenly to edge of each. Bake in 250°F (120°C) oven for about 45 minutes until dry. Turn oven off. Let stand in oven with door ajar until cool. Remove meringues to wire racks and discard parchment paper.

Filling: Heat chips and water in small heavy saucepan on lowest heat, stirring often, until chips are almost melted. Do not overheat. Remove from heat. Stir until smooth. Divide and spread over 2 meringues.

Beat whipping cream, sugar and vanilla in large bowl until stiff peaks form. Divide and spread over all 3 meringues.

Carefully place 1 meringue with chocolate on serving plate. Spoon 1/2 of sliced strawberries evenly over whipped cream. Place second meringue with chocolate on top. Spoon remaining strawberries evenly over whipped cream. Place third meringue on top.

Garnish with strawberries and chocolate curls. Chill for 4 to 5 hours before serving. Serves 8.

1 serving: 612 Calories; 37.2 g Total Fat (11.1 g Mono, 1.3 g Poly, 22.9 g Sat); 110 mg Cholesterol; 70 g Carbohydrate; 3 g Fibre; 6 g Protein; 78 mg Sodium

Pictured on page 53.

Also known as Death By Chocolate, this is a wonderful crowd-pleaser. Recipe can be cut in half for a smaller group.

Truffle Trifle

Box of chocolate cake mix (2 layer size)	1	1
Coffee-flavoured liqueur (such as Kahlúa) or 1/2 cup (125 mL) cold prepared strong coffee	2/3 cup	150 mL
Boxes of instant chocolate pudding powder (4 serving size, each)	2	2
Milk	4 cups	1 L
Frozen whipped topping, thawed	4 cups	1 L
Chocolate-covered crispy toffee bars (such as Heath or Skor), 1 1/2 oz. (39 g) each, crushed	6	6
Chocolate curls (see Note, page 57), for garnish		

Prepare cake mix according to package directions. Divide and spread evenly in 2 greased 8 inch (20 cm) round pans. Bake as directed. Let stand in pans for 5 minutes before inverting onto wire racks to cool completely.

Transfer first cake layer to cutting board. Drizzle with 1/2 of liqueur. Cut into 1 inch (2.5 cm) cubes. Transfer to 6 quart (6 L) glass trifle bowl. Transfer second cake layer to cutting board. Drizzle with remaining liqueur. Cut into 1 inch (2.5 cm) cubes. Set aside.

Beat pudding powder and milk in medium bowl until slightly thickened. Pour 1/2 of pudding over cake in bowl.

Spread 1/2 of whipped topping evenly over pudding. Sprinkle 1/2 of crushed toffee bars over whipped topping. Repeat layering with remaining cake cubes, pudding, whipped topping and crushed toffee bars.

Garnish with chocolate curls. Chill for 1 hour. Serves 20.

1 serving: 303 Calories; 11.2 g Total Fat (1.7 g Mono, 0.4 g Poly, 4.6 g Sat); 9 mg Cholesterol; 45 g Carbohydrate; 0 g Fibre; 4 g Protein; 434 mg Sodium

Pictured on page 55.

Left: Mango Raspberry Trifles, page 56
Right: Truffle Trifle, above

Mango and fresh raspberries make this a very colourful dessert. Assemble in individual wine glasses and serve after a special meal.

Mango Raspberry Trifles

Orange-flavoured liqueur (such as Grand Marnier)	2 tbsp.	30 mL
Orange juice	1/4 cup	60 mL
Mascarpone cheese	1 1/3 cups	325 mL
Icing (confectioner's) sugar	1/3 cup	75 mL
Giant ladyfingers	8	8
Cans of sliced mango with syrup (14 oz., 398 mL, each), drained and sliced diagonally	2	2
Fresh raspberries	1 1/3 cups	325 mL

Combine liqueur and orange juice in small bowl.

Beat mascarpone cheese and icing sugar in separate small bowl until smooth.

Break each ladyfinger in half, for a total of 16 pieces. Dip 8 pieces into orange juice mixture. Place 2 pieces in each of 4 serving glasses. Divide and spoon 1/2 of mango over ladyfingers. Divide and spoon 1/2 of cheese mixture over mango. Divide and spoon 1/2 of raspberries over cheese mixture. Dip remaining ladyfinger pieces in orange juice mixture. Repeat layering with remaining ladyfinger pieces, mango and cheese mixture. Garnish with remaining raspberries. Chill. Serves 4.

1 serving: 560 Calories; 32.1 g Total Fat (9.3 g Mono, 1.7 g Poly, 19 g Sat); 210 mg Cholesterol; 57 g Carbohydrate; 4 g Fibre; 11 g Protein; 293 mg Sodium

Pictured on page 55.

Pure bliss. Soft and creamy. Do not freeze.

Chocolate Mousse

Semi-sweet chocolate chips	1 cup	250 mL
Egg yolks (large)	4	4
Vanilla	1/2 tsp.	2 mL
Egg whites (large), room temperature (see Safety Tip)	4	4
Icing (confectioner's) sugar	1/4 cup	60 mL
Whipping cream (or 1 envelope of dessert topping)	1 cup	250 mL

(continued on next page)

Whipped cream, for garnish
Chocolate filigrees (see Note), for garnish
Chocolate curls (see Note), for garnish

Heat chips in heavy medium saucepan on lowest heat, stirring often, until chips are almost melted. Do not overheat. Remove from heat. Stir until smooth. Add egg yolks and vanilla. Stir well. Transfer to large bowl.

Beat egg whites in medium bowl until soft peaks form. Add icing sugar, 1 tbsp. (15 mL) at a time while beating, until stiff peaks form.

Using same beaters, beat first amount of whipping cream in small bowl until stiff peaks form or prepare dessert topping according to package directions.

Fold 2 tbsp. (30 mL) egg white mixture into chocolate mixture to lighten. Fold in remaining egg white mixture until no white streaks remain. Fold in whipped cream until well combined. Divide and spoon into 8 individual bowls or goblets. Chill for at least 6 hours. Garnish with whipped cream, chocolate filigrees and chocolate curls. Makes 4 3/4 cups (1.2 L) mousse. Serves 8.

1 serving: 255 Calories; 19.3 g Total Fat (6.1 g Mono, 0.9 g Poly, 11 g Sat); 144 mg Cholesterol; 19 g Carbohydrate; 1 g Fibre; 5 g Protein; 45 mg Sodium

Pictured below.

Safety Tip: This recipe uses uncooked eggs. Make sure to use fresh, clean Grade A eggs. Keep chilled and consume the same day it is prepared. Always discard leftovers. Pregnant women, young children or the elderly are not advised to eat anything containing raw egg.

note

To make chocolate filigrees, tape parchment (or waxed) paper onto rolling pin. Drizzle melted chocolate back and forth over curve of rolling pin in desired designs. Let stand until set. Carefully peel paper from chocolate design.

note

To make chocolate curls, peel room temperature chocolate firmly along its length with sharp vegetable peeler. For narrower curls, use flat underside of peeler.

This creamy dish somehow became known as Sex In A Pan—no doubt miscopied from Six in a Pan. Garnish with shaved chocolate.

Six Layer Dessert

CRUST

Hard margarine (or butter)	1/2 cup	125 mL
All-purpose flour	1 cup	250 mL
Finely chopped nuts (your favourite), optional	1/2 cup	125 mL
Granulated sugar	2 tbsp.	30 mL

LAYERS

Block of cream cheese, softened	8 oz.	250 g
Icing (confectioner's) sugar	1 cup	250 mL
Whipping cream (or 1 envelope of dessert topping)	1 cup	250 mL
Box of instant chocolate pudding powder (4 serving size)	1	1
Milk	1 1/2 cups	375 mL
Box of instant vanilla pudding powder (4 serving size)	1	1
Milk	1 1/2 cups	375 mL

Crust: Melt margarine in medium saucepan. Remove from heat. Add flour, nuts and sugar. Stir well. Press firmly in ungreased 9 x 13 inch (22 x 33 cm) pan. Bake in 325°F (160°C) oven for about 15 minutes until golden. Let stand in pan on wire rack until cooled completely.

Layers: Beat cream cheese and icing sugar in medium bowl until smooth. Spread evenly over crust.

Beat whipping cream in small bowl until stiff peaks form. Spread 1/2 of whipped cream evenly over cream cheese layer.

Beat chocolate pudding powder and first amount of milk in medium bowl for about 2 minutes until slightly thickened. Spread evenly over whipped cream layer. Let stand until set.

Beat vanilla pudding powder and second amount of milk in medium bowl for about 2 minutes until slightly thickened. Spread evenly over chocolate pudding layer. Let stand until set. Spread remaining whipped cream evenly over vanilla pudding layer. Chill overnight. Cuts into 15 pieces.

1 piece: 309 Calories; 18.4 g Total Fat (7.6 g Mono, 1.1 g Poly, 8.8 g Sat); 40 mg Cholesterol; 33 g Carbohydrate; trace Fibre; 4 g Protein; 352 mg Sodium

Pictured on page 59.

Top: Raspberry Dessert, page 60
Centre: Six Layer Dessert, above
Bottom: Glimmering Slice, page 61

Mix and match various combinations of strawberry or raspberry jelly powder and frozen strawberries or raspberries. All are delicious!

Raspberry Dessert

GRAHAM CRUMB CRUST		
Hard margarine (or butter), melted	1/2 cup	125 mL
Graham cracker crumbs	2 cups	500 mL
Brown sugar, packed	1/4 cup	60 mL
SECOND LAYER		
Block of cream cheese, softened	8 oz.	250 g
Icing (confectioner's) sugar	1/2 cup	125 mL
Vanilla	1 tsp.	5 mL
Salt	1/2 tsp.	2 mL
THIRD LAYER		
Boiling water	1 1/4 cups	300 mL
Boxes of strawberry-flavoured jelly powder (gelatin), 3 oz. (85 g) each	2	2
Granulated sugar	1/4 cup	60 mL
Package of frozen raspberries in syrup, thawed	15 oz.	425 g
Lemon juice	1 tsp.	5 mL
TOP LAYER		
Whipping cream	2 cups	500 mL
Icing (confectioner's) sugar	1/4 cup	60 mL
Vanilla	1 tsp.	5 mL

Graham Crumb Crust: Combine margarine, graham crumbs and brown sugar in medium bowl. Stir well. Reserve 1/2 cup (125 mL) crumb mixture for garnish. Press remaining crumb mixture firmly in ungreased 9 x 13 inch (22 x 33 cm) pan. Bake in 350ºF (175ºC) oven for 10 minutes. Let stand in pan on wire rack until cooled completely.

Second Layer: Beat all 4 ingredients in small bowl until smooth. Spread evenly over graham crust.

Third Layer: Pour boiling water into separate small bowl. Add jelly powder and sugar. Stir until dissolved.

Add raspberries with syrup and lemon juice. Stir. Chill, stirring and scraping side of bowl every 10 minutes, until jelly mixture starts to thicken. Spread evenly over cream cheese layer. Chill until set.

Top Layer: Beat all 3 ingredients in small bowl until stiff peaks form. Spread evenly over jelly layer. Sprinkle with reserved crumbs. Chill. Cuts into 15 pieces.

(continued on next page)

1 piece: 395 Calories; 24.3 g Total Fat (9.6 g Mono, 1.4 g Poly, 12 g Sat); 57 mg Cholesterol;
42 g Carbohydrate; 2 g Fibre; 4 g Protein; 318 mg Sodium

Pictured on page 59.

Glimmering Slice

This looks as spectacular as it tastes!

GRAHAM CRUMB CRUST
Hard margarine (or butter), melted	1/2 cup	125 mL
Graham cracker crumbs	2 cups	500 mL
Brown sugar, packed	1/4 cup	60 mL

SECOND LAYER
Envelope of unflavoured gelatin (1 tbsp., 15 mL)	1	1
Cold water	1/4 cup	60 mL
Cold water	1/2 cup	125 mL
Lemon juice	1/2 cup	125 mL
Can of sweetened condensed milk	11 oz.	300 mL

THIRD LAYER
Boiling water	3 cups	750 mL
Boxes of raspberry-flavoured jelly powder (gelatin), 3 oz. (85 g) each	2	2

Graham Crumb Crust: Combine margarine, graham crumbs and brown sugar in medium bowl. Stir well. Press firmly in ungreased 9 x 13 inch (22 x 33 cm) pan. Bake in 350°F (175°C) oven for 10 minutes. Let stand in pan on wire rack until cooled completely.

Second Layer: Sprinkle gelatin over first amount of cold water in small saucepan. Let stand for 1 minute. Heat and stir on low until gelatin is dissolved. Remove from heat.

Combine second amount of cold water, lemon juice and condensed milk in small bowl. Add gelatin mixture. Beat well. Spread evenly over graham crust.

Third Layer: Pour boiling water into separate small bowl. Add jelly powder. Stir until jelly powder is dissolved. Chill, stirring and scraping side of bowl every 10 minutes, until jelly mixture starts to thicken. Spread evenly over lemon mixture. Chill until set. Cuts into 15 pieces.

1 piece: 254 Calories; 9.9 g Total Fat (5.4 g Mono, 0.9 g Poly, 3 g Sat); 9 mg Cholesterol; 39 g Carbohydrate; trace Fibre; 4 g Protein; 212 mg Sodium

Pictured on page 59.

Top with your favourite fruit to create a colourful presentation.

Fruit Pizza

CRUST

All-purpose flour	1 1/4 cups	300 mL
Brown sugar, packed	1/3 cup	75 mL
Icing (confectioner's) sugar	3 tbsp.	50 mL
Hard margarine (or butter), cut up	2/3 cup	150 mL

TOPPING

Blocks of cream cheese (4 oz., 125 g, each), softened	3	3
Granulated sugar	1/2 cup	125 mL
Vanilla	1 tsp.	5 mL
Variety of fresh fruit (such as strawberries, kiwifruit, peaches and blueberries), sliced		

APRICOT GLAZE

Apricot jam (or orange marmalade)	1/4 cup	60 mL
Water	1 tbsp.	15 mL

Crust: Combine flour, brown sugar and icing sugar in medium bowl. Cut in margarine until mixture resembles fine crumbs. Press mixture together to form smooth ball. Press firmly in ungreased 12 inch (30 cm) pizza pan. Bake in 350°F (175°C) oven for 10 to 15 minutes until golden. Let stand in pan on wire rack until cooled completely.

Topping: Beat cream cheese, sugar and vanilla in large bowl until smooth. Spread evenly over crust. Arrange fruit in attractive pattern over cream cheese mixture.

Apricot Glaze: Combine apricot jam and water in small bowl. Press through sieve into separate small bowl. Brush lightly over fruit. Chill. Cuts into 12 wedges.

1 wedge: 359 Calories; 22 g Total Fat (10.1 g Mono, 1.5 g Poly, 9.1 g Sat); 34 mg Cholesterol; 38 g Carbohydrate; 2 g Fibre; 4 g Protein; 225 mg Sodium

Pictured on page 63.

Peanut Ice Cream Treat

Butterscotch (or caramel) ice cream topping	1/3 cup	75 mL
Chocolate (or fudge) ice cream topping	1/3 cup	75 mL
Commercial chocolate crumb crust (9 inch, 22 cm, diameter)	1	1
Vanilla (or butterscotch ripple) ice cream, softened	4 cups	1 L
Roasted unsalted peanuts, chopped	1/2 cup	125 mL
Butterscotch (or caramel) ice cream topping, for garnish		
Chocolate (or fudge) ice cream topping, for garnish		

Spoon alternating teaspoonfuls (using 1 tsp., 5 mL, for each) of first amounts of butterscotch and chocolate toppings over crust. Freeze for 20 minutes.

Spread ice cream evenly over crust.

Sprinkle peanuts over ice cream. Cover with plastic wrap. Freeze for at least 8 hours or overnight until firm.

Drizzle second amounts of butterscotch and chocolate toppings over peanuts. Freeze until firm. Cuts into 8 wedges.

1 wedge: 425 Calories; 23.1 g Total Fat (9.2 g Mono, 4.4 g Poly, 8.1 g Sat); 33 mg Cholesterol; 52 g Carbohydrate; 1 g Fibre; 7 g Protein; 313 mg Sodium

Pictured on page 65 and on back cover.

Can it get any better than this for banana split lovers?

note

To toast nuts, place in single layer in ungreased shallow pan. Bake in 350°F (175°C) oven for 5 to 8 minutes, stirring or shaking often, until desired doneness.

chocolate dips

Heat and stir 2 semi-sweet chocolate baking squares (1 oz., 28 g, each) in small heavy saucepan on lowest heat until chocolate is almost melted. Do not overheat. Remove from heat. Stir until smooth. Dip bottom half of each of 18 banana chips in chocolate, allowing excess to drip back into saucepan. Place chips on parchment paper-lined baking sheet. Chill until set. Makes 18 dips.

Banana Macadamia Sundaes

CARAMEL SAUCE

Brown sugar, packed	1/2 cup	125 mL
Hard margarine (or butter)	1/3 cup	75 mL
Whipping cream	1/3 cup	75 mL
Vanilla	1/2 tsp.	2 mL

CHOCOLATE FUDGE SAUCE

Whipping cream	1/2 cup	125 mL
Semi-sweet chocolate bar (3 1/2 oz., 100 g), chopped	1	1
Large marshmallows, chopped	6	6
Chocolate ice cream, approximately	3 cups	750 mL
Medium bananas	6	6
Whipped cream	1 1/2 cups	375 mL
Coarsely chopped macadamia nuts, toasted (see Note)	3/4 cup	175 mL
Chocolate Dips, for garnish	18	18

Caramel Sauce: Heat and stir all 4 ingredients in medium saucepan on medium until boiling. Boil, without stirring, for about 5 minutes until smooth and slightly thickened. Remove from heat. Makes about 2/3 cup (150 mL) Caramel Sauce.

Chocolate Fudge Sauce: Heat and stir whipping cream, chocolate and marshmallow in medium saucepan on medium until smooth. Makes about 1 cup (250 mL) fudge sauce.

In each of six 1 1/2 cup (375 mL) float glasses or wine goblets, layer as follows:

1. 1 scoop ice cream (1/4 cup, 60 mL)
2. 1/2 banana, sliced
3. 1 1/2 tbsp. (25 mL) Caramel Sauce
4. 2 tbsp. (30 mL) whipped cream
5. 1 tbsp. (15 mL) macadamia nuts
6. 1 scoop ice cream (1/4 cup, 60 mL)
7. 1/2 banana, sliced
8. 2 1/2 tbsp. (37 mL) Chocolate Fudge Sauce
9. 2 tbsp. (30 mL) whipped cream
10. 1 tbsp. (15 mL) macadamia nuts

Garnish each with 3 Chocolate Dips. Makes 6 sundaes.

1 sundae: 832 Calories; 56 g Total Fat (25.6 g Mono, 2.4 g Poly, 25 g Sat); 101 mg Cholesterol; 86 g Carbohydrate; 4 g Fibre; 7 g Protein; 217 mg Sodium

Pictured on page 67 and on back cover.

Pears poached in maple syrup and port wine, with a hint of cinnamon and cloves. The perfect treat on a cold day.

Poached Maple Pears

Fresh firm medium pears	4	4
Port wine	1 cup	250 mL
Orange juice	1/2 cup	125 mL
Maple (or maple-flavoured) syrup	1/3 cup	75 mL
Cinnamon stick (4 inch, 10 cm, length)	1	1
Whole cloves	6	6

Fresh mint leaves, for garnish

Carefully remove cores from pears using apple corer, leaving pear whole. Peel pears.

Combine next 5 ingredients in medium saucepan. Lay pears on sides in wine mixture. Bring to a boil on medium. Reduce heat to medium-low. Simmer, uncovered, for 15 to 20 minutes, turning pears occasionally, until softened and evenly coloured. Remove pears using slotted spoon. Cover to keep warm. Remove and discard cinnamon stick and cloves. Bring wine mixture to a boil on medium. Boil, uncovered, for 10 to 15 minutes until reduced to about 3/4 cup (175 mL).

Slice pears evenly, making 6 or 7 cuts from large end of pear to within 1/2 inch (12 mm) of small end. Place 1 pear, large end down, on each of 4 dessert plates. Fan pear slices out slightly. Drizzle with wine mixture. Garnish with mint leaves. Serves 4.

1 serving: 177 Calories; 0.2 g Total Fat (0 g Mono, 0 g Poly, 0 g Sat); 0 mg Cholesterol; 35 g Carbohydrate; 3 g Fibre; 1 g Protein; 9 mg Sodium

Pictured on page 69.

Top Left: Brandied Peaches, page 70
Top Right: Baked Apples, page 70
Centre: Poached Maple Pears, above

variations

Add 1 tsp. (5 mL) ground cinnamon to brown sugar. Stir well. Proceed as directed.

Remove apples from oven about halfway through baking time. Spoon mincemeat into cavities. Bake as directed.

variation

Use only 2 tbsp. (30 mL) reserved juice and substitute Grand Marnier (orange-flavoured liqueur) for the brandy.

Baked Apples

Medium cooking apples (such as McIntosh)	4	4
Brown sugar, packed	1 cup	250 mL
Hard margarine (or butter), softened	2 tsp.	10 mL

Carefully remove cores from apples using apple corer, leaving apples whole (with peel). Arrange in ungreased 8 × 8 inch (20 × 20 cm) pan. Divide and pack brown sugar into centre of each apple. Spoon 1/2 tsp. (2 mL) margarine over brown sugar. Bake in 350°F (175°C) oven for 25 to 35 minutes until apples are tender. Transfer 1 apple to each of 4 individual bowls. Spoon sauce from pan over apples. Serves 4.

1 serving: 317 Calories; 2.4 g Total Fat (1.3 g Mono, 0.3 g Poly, 0.5 g Sat); 0 mg Cholesterol; 78 g Carbohydrate; 3 g Fibre; 0 g Protein; 45 mg Sodium

Pictured on page 69.

Brandied Peaches

Cans of peach halves in pear juice (14 oz., 398 mL, each)	2	2
Brown sugar, packed	2/3 cup	150 mL
Hard margarine (or butter)	2 tbsp.	30 mL
Ground cinnamon	1/4 tsp.	1 mL
Lemon juice	1 tsp.	5 mL
Brandy flavouring (or 1/4 cup, 60 mL, brandy)	1 tsp.	5 mL
Almond flavouring (optional)	1/4 tsp.	1 mL
Vanilla ice cream	6 cups	1.5 L

Drain peaches, reserving juice. Chop peaches. Transfer to medium saucepan. Add reserved juice. Add next 6 ingredients. Bring to a boil on medium. Reduce heat to medium-low. Simmer, uncovered, for 5 minutes, stirring occasionally.

Scoop 1/2 cup (125 mL) ice cream into each of 12 individual dishes. Divide and spoon brandied peaches over top. Serves 12.

1 serving: 237 Calories; 9.6 g Total Fat (3.5 g Mono, 0.5 g Poly, 5.1 g Sat); 31 mg Cholesterol; 37 g Carbohydrate; 1 g Fibre; 3 g Protein; 86 mg Sodium

Pictured on page 69.

Brown Betty

*An all-time favourite. Good hot or cold.
Even better served with ice cream.*

Peeled, cored and sliced cooking apples (such as McIntosh)	6 cups	1.5 L
Granulated sugar	3/4 cup	175 mL
STREUSEL TOPPING		
All-purpose flour	1 1/4 cups	300 mL
Brown sugar, packed	3/4 cup	175 mL
Salt	1/2 tsp.	2 mL
Hard margarine (or butter), cut up	1/2 cup	125 mL

Place apple slices in ungreased shallow 3 quart (3 L) casserole. Sprinkle sugar over top.

Streusel Topping: Combine flour, brown sugar and salt in medium bowl. Cut in margarine until mixture resembles coarse crumbs. Scatter evenly over apple. Press down lightly. Bake, uncovered, in 375°F (190°C) oven for about 40 minutes until apple is tender. Serves 8.

1 serving: 392 Calories; 12.5 g Total Fat (7.9 g Mono, 1.4 g Poly, 2.6 g Sat); 0 mg Cholesterol; 70 g Carbohydrate; 2 g Fibre; 2 g Protein; 299 mg Sodium

Pictured below.

rhubarb betty

Omit apple and use same amount of sliced fresh or frozen rhubarb, adding 1/2 cup (125 mL) more sugar. Better yet, add a few raisins and omit the extra sugar. Bake as directed.

fresh fruit betty

Omit apple and use fresh peaches, peeled and sliced, or fresh apricots, quartered. Bake as directed.

A treat everyone looks forward to! Freezes well.

Nanaimo Bars

BOTTOM LAYER

Hard margarine (or butter)	1/2 cup	125 mL
Cocoa, sifted if lumpy	1/3 cup	75 mL
Granulated sugar	1/4 cup	60 mL
Large egg, fork-beaten	1	1
Graham cracker crumbs	1 3/4 cups	425 mL
Fine (or medium unsweetened) coconut	3/4 cup	175 mL
Finely chopped walnuts	1/2 cup	125 mL

MIDDLE LAYER

Icing (confectioner's) sugar	2 cups	500 mL
Hard margarine (or butter), softened	1/2 cup	125 mL
Milk	3 tbsp.	50 mL
Vanilla custard powder	2 tbsp.	30 mL

TOP LAYER

Semi-sweet chocolate chips	2/3 cup	150 mL
Hard margarine (or butter)	2 tbsp.	30 mL

Bottom Layer: Heat and stir margarine, cocoa and sugar in heavy medium saucepan on medium-low until smooth. Add egg. Stir until thickened. Remove from heat.

Add graham crumbs, coconut and walnuts. Stir well. Press firmly in ungreased 9 x 9 inch (22 x 22 cm) pan.

Middle Layer: Beat all 4 ingredients in medium bowl until smooth. Spread evenly over bottom layer.

Top Layer: Heat chips and margarine in small heavy saucepan on lowest heat, stirring often, until chips are almost melted. Do not overheat. Remove from heat. Stir until smooth. Cool slightly. Spread evenly over middle layer. Chill until top layer is set. Cuts into 36 squares.

1 square: 153 Calories; 10.1 g Total Fat (4.9 g Mono, 1.4 g Poly, 3.3 g Sat); 9 mg Cholesterol; 16 g Carbohydrate; 1 g Fibre; 2 g Protein; 106 mg Sodium

Pictured on page 73.

Top Left: Mars Bars Squares, page 74
Top Right And Bottom: Nanaimo Bars, above
Centre Right: Chocolate Crisps, page 74

Crisp and chocolaty. For a pretty contrast, drizzle melted white chocolate over top before cutting.

Mars Bars Squares

Mars candy bars (1 3/4 oz., 50 g, each, black and red label), chopped	4	4
Hard margarine (or butter)	1/2 cup	125 mL
Crisp rice cereal	3 cups	750 mL
Semi-sweet chocolate chips	1 cup	250 mL
Hard margarine (or butter)	1/4 cup	60 mL

Heat and stir candy bar pieces and first amount of margarine in large heavy saucepan on low until smooth. Remove from heat.

Add cereal. Stir until coated. Press evenly in greased or foil-lined 9 x 9 inch (22 x 22 cm) pan.

Heat chips and second amount of margarine in small heavy saucepan on lowest heat, stirring often, until chips are melted. Spread evenly over cereal mixture in pan. Chill. Cuts into 36 squares.

1 square: 92 Calories; 6.4 g Total Fat (3.5 g Mono, 0.5 g Poly, 2.1 g Sat); 1 mg Cholesterol; 9 g Carbohydrate; trace Fibre; 1 g Protein; 86 mg Sodium

Pictured on page 73.

Even the kids can make these. Fast and easy. Tastes like candy!

Chocolate Crisps

Smooth peanut butter	1 cup	250 mL
Liquid honey	3/4 cup	175 mL
Semi-sweet chocolate chips	1 cup	250 mL
Crisp rice cereal	3 cups	750 mL
Salted peanuts	1 cup	250 mL

Heat peanut butter and honey in large heavy saucepan on lowest heat, stirring often, until melted. Bring to a gentle boil. Remove from heat.

Add chips. Stir until smooth.

Add cereal and peanuts. Stir until coated. Press firmly in greased or foil-lined 9 x 9 inch (22 x 22 cm) pan. Chill until firm. Cuts into 36 squares.

1 square: 130 Calories; 7.5 g Total Fat (3.4 g Mono, 1.8 g Poly, 2 g Sat); 0 mg Cholesterol; 15 g Carbohydrate; 1 g Fibre; 3 g Protein; 96 mg Sodium

Pictured on page 73.

Shortbread

A favourite, no-fail recipe for shortbread.

All-purpose flour	2 cups	500 mL
Icing (confectioner's) sugar (see Note)	1/2 cup	125 mL
Butter (not margarine), cut up	1 cup	250 mL

Combine flour and icing sugar in large bowl. Cut in butter until mixture resembles fine crumbs. Press mixture together to form smooth ball. Press evenly in ungreased 9 x 9 inch (22 x 22 cm) pan. Prick entire surface of dough with fork through to bottom of pan. Bake in 300°F (150°C) oven for 50 to 60 minutes until just golden. Let stand in pan on wire rack for 5 minutes. Cuts into 36 squares.

1 square: 81 Calories; 5.5 g Total Fat (1.6 g Mono, 0.2 g Poly, 3.4 g Sat); 15 mg Cholesterol; 7 g Carbohydrate; trace Fibre; 1 g Protein; 55 mg Sodium

Pictured below.

scotch shortbread

Omit icing sugar. Use same amount of granulated sugar.

The perfect ending to an evening meal.

Midnight Mints

BOTTOM LAYER		
Hard margarine (or butter)	1/2 cup	125 mL
Cocoa, sifted if lumpy	1/3 cup	75 mL
Granulated sugar	1/4 cup	60 mL
Large egg, fork-beaten	1	1
Graham cracker crumbs	1 3/4 cups	425 mL
Fine coconut	3/4 cup	175 mL
Finely chopped walnuts	1/2 cup	125 mL
MIDDLE LAYER		
Icing (confectioner's) sugar	2 cups	500 mL
Hard margarine (or butter), softened	1/3 cup	75 mL
Milk	3 tbsp.	50 mL
Peppermint flavouring	1 tsp.	5 mL
Green liquid (or paste) food colouring		
TOP LAYER		
Semi-sweet chocolate chips	2/3 cup	150 mL
Hard margarine (or butter)	2 tbsp.	30 mL

Bottom Layer: Heat margarine, cocoa and sugar in large heavy saucepan on low, stirring often, until sugar is dissolved. Add egg. Stir until thickened. Remove from heat.

Add graham crumbs, coconut and walnuts. Stir well. Press firmly in ungreased 9 x 9 inch (22 x 22 cm) pan.

Middle Layer: Beat first 4 ingredients in medium bowl until smooth, adding more milk or icing sugar as necessary until spreading consistency. Add enough food colouring until pale green. Spread evenly over bottom layer.

Top Layer: Heat chips and margarine in small heavy saucepan on lowest heat, stirring often, until chips are almost melted. Do not overheat. Remove from heat. Stir until smooth. Cool slightly. Spread evenly over middle layer. Chill until top layer is set. Cuts into 36 squares.

1 square: 142 Calories; 9.1 g Total Fat (4.3 g Mono, 1.3 g Poly, 3.1 g Sat); 6 mg Cholesterol; 15 g Carbohydrate; 1 g Fibre; 1 g Protein; 90 mg Sodium

Pictured on page 77.

Millionaire means rich—exactly what these squares are!

Millionaire Squares

BOTTOM LAYER		
Hard margarine (or butter)	1/2 cup	125 mL
Finely crushed crisp oatmeal cookies (such as Dad's)	2 cups	500 mL
FILLING		
Semi-sweet chocolate baking squares (1 oz., 28 g, each), chopped (or 1/2 cup, 125 mL, chocolate chips)	3	3
Hard margarine (or butter)	1/2 cup	125 mL
Large egg	1	1
Icing (confectioner's) sugar	2 cups	500 mL
Chopped walnuts (optional)	1/2 cup	125 mL

Bottom Layer: Melt margarine in medium saucepan. Remove from heat. Add crushed cookies. Stir well. Reserve 1/4 cup (60 mL) crumb mixture for topping. Press remaining mixture firmly in greased 8 × 8 inch (20 × 20 cm) pan. Bake in 350°F (175°C) oven for 5 minutes. Let stand in pan on wire rack until cooled completely.

Filling: Heat chocolate and margarine in heavy medium saucepan on lowest heat, stirring often, until chocolate is almost melted. Do not overheat. Remove from heat. Stir until smooth. Add egg. Beat. Add icing sugar, 2 tbsp. (30 mL) at a time while beating, until smooth, adding more icing sugar as necessary until spreading consistency.

Add walnuts. Stir. Spread evenly over bottom layer. Sprinkle reserved crumb mixture over top. Chill until firm. Cuts into 25 squares.

1 square: 169 Calories; 10.6 g Total Fat (6.4 g Mono, 1.1 g Poly, 2.5 g Sat); 9 mg Cholesterol; 19 g Carbohydrate; trace Fibre; 1 g Protein; 129 mg Sodium

Pictured on page 79.

Top Left: Fudgy Macaroons, page 80
Top Right: Millionaire Squares, above
Bottom Right: Butterscotch Confetti, page 81
Bottom Left: Swirl Squares, page 80

The swirl is made with chocolate chips. No need to ice these. The recipe is easily doubled.

Swirl Squares

Hard margarine (or butter), softened	1/2 cup	125 mL
Brown sugar, packed	1/2 cup	125 mL
Granulated sugar	1/4 cup	60 mL
Vanilla	1/2 tsp.	2 mL
Large egg	1	1
All-purpose flour	1 1/8 cups	280 mL
Baking soda	1/2 tsp.	2 mL
Salt	1/2 tsp.	2 mL
Chopped walnuts	1/2 cup	125 mL
Semi-sweet chocolate chips	1 cup	250 mL

Beat first 5 ingredients in large bowl until light and creamy.

Combine flour, baking soda and salt in small bowl. Add to margarine mixture. Stir until smooth.

Add walnuts. Stir. Spread evenly in greased 9 x 9 inch (22 x 22 cm) pan.

Scatter chips over top. Bake in 375°F (190°C) oven for 1 to 2 minutes until chips are very soft. Remove from oven. Swirl knife through batter to create marble effect. Return to oven. Bake for about 20 minutes until firm and wooden pick inserted in centre comes out clean. Let stand in pan on wire rack until cool. Cuts into 36 squares.

1 square: 94 Calories; 5.4 g Total Fat (2.5 g Mono, 1 g Poly, 1.5 g Sat); 6 mg Cholesterol; 11 g Carbohydrate; 1 g Fibre; 1 g Protein; 86 mg Sodium

Pictured on page 79.

Crunchy butterscotch treats. Similar taste to brown sugar fudge.

Fudgy Macaroons

Granulated sugar	1 1/2 cups	375 mL
Evaporated milk	1 cup	250 mL
Hard margarine (or butter)	1/4 cup	60 mL
Butterscotch chips	2 cups	500 mL
Vanilla	1 tsp.	5 mL

(continued on next page)

Cornflakes cereal, lightly packed	4 cups	1 L
Medium unsweetened coconut	2 1/2 cups	625 mL
Chopped walnuts	1 cup	250 mL

Heat and stir sugar, evaporated milk and margarine in large heavy saucepan on medium. Bring to a rolling boil. Immediately remove from heat.

Add chips and vanilla. Stir until smooth.

Add cereal, coconut and walnuts. Stir until coated. Press firmly in greased or foil-lined 9 × 9 inch (22 × 22 cm) pan. Chill until firm. Cuts into 36 squares.

1 square: 198 Calories; 8.6 g Total Fat (1.8 g Mono, 1.6 g Poly, 4.6 g Sat); 3 mg Cholesterol; 29 g Carbohydrate; 1 g Fibre; 3 g Protein; 138 mg Sodium

Pictured on page 79.

Butterscotch Confetti

Butterscotch chips	1 cup	250 mL
Smooth peanut butter	1/2 cup	125 mL
Hard margarine (or butter)	1/4 cup	60 mL
Package of miniature multi-coloured marshmallows	8 oz.	250 g

Heat first 3 ingredients in large heavy saucepan on lowest heat, stirring often, until chips are almost melted. Do not overheat. Remove from heat. Stir until smooth. Let stand until bottom of saucepan is cool enough to touch.

Add marshmallows. Stir until coated. Press firmly in greased or foil-lined 9 × 9 inch (22 × 22 cm) pan. Chill until firm. Cuts into 36 squares.

1 square: 73 Calories; 3.4 g Total Fat (1.8 g Mono, 0.7 g Poly, 0.7 g Sat); 0 mg Cholesterol; 10 g Carbohydrate; trace Fibre; 1 g Protein; 39 mg Sodium

Pictured on page 79.

There is no excuse not to have this treat on hand. Freezes well. Colourful!

variation

Line bottom of pan with whole graham crackers first. Proceed as directed in recipe.

variation

Add 1/2 cup (125 mL) chopped walnuts and/or 1/2 cup (125 mL) medium unsweetened coconut to recipe ingredients.

Make these when you're looking for something a little different.

Tweed Squares

Hard margarine (or butter), softened	1/2 cup	125 mL
Granulated sugar	2/3 cup	150 mL
All-purpose flour	1 1/3 cups	325 mL
Baking powder	2 tsp.	10 mL
Salt	1/2 tsp.	2 mL
Milk	1/2 cup	125 mL
Egg whites (large), room temperature	2	2
Semi-sweet chocolate baking squares (1 oz., 28 g, each), finely grated	2	2
VANILLA ICING		
Icing (confectioner's) sugar	1 1/2 cups	375 mL
Hard margarine (or butter), softened	3 tbsp.	50 mL
Water	1 1/2 tbsp.	25 mL
Vanilla	1/2 tsp.	2 mL
Semi-sweet chocolate baking squares (1 oz., 28 g, each), chopped	2	2
Hard margarine (or butter)	1 tbsp.	15 mL

Beat margarine and sugar in large bowl until light and creamy.

Combine flour, baking powder and salt in small bowl. Add flour mixture to margarine mixture in 2 additions, alternating with milk in 1 addition, beginning and ending with flour mixture.

Beat egg whites in separate small bowl until stiff peaks form. Fold into batter until no white streaks remain.

Fold in grated chocolate. Spread evenly in greased 9 x 9 inch (22 x 22 cm) pan. Bake in 350°F (175°C) oven for about 35 minutes until golden. Let stand in pan on wire rack until cooled completely.

Vanilla Icing: Beat first 4 ingredients in small bowl until smooth, adding more water or icing sugar as necessary until spreading consistency. Spread evenly over first layer. Let stand for at least 1 hour until set.

(continued on next page)

Heat chocolate and margarine in small heavy saucepan on lowest heat, stirring often, until chocolate is almost melted. Do not overheat. Remove from heat. Stir until smooth. Cool slightly. Spread evenly over icing. Chill until top layer is set. Cuts into 36 squares.

1 square: 107 Calories; 5 g Total Fat (2.9 g Mono, 0.4 g Poly, 1.4 g Sat); 0 mg Cholesterol; 15 g Carbohydrate; trace Fibre; 1 g Protein; 105 mg Sodium

Pictured below.

Top: Tweed Squares, page 82
Bottom: Chocolate Roll, page 84

A colourful confection with a smooth texture. After a few slices are cut, you can pop it back in the refrigerator or freezer.

variation

Reduce coconut to 1/4 cup (60 mL). Add with rest of ingredients. Mix well. Press firmly in greased or foil-lined 8 x 8 inch (20 x 20 cm) pan. Cuts into 25 squares.

Chocolate Roll

Semi-sweet chocolate chips	1 cup	250 mL
Hard margarine (or butter)	2 tbsp.	30 mL
Miniature multi-coloured marshmallows	2 1/2 cups	625 mL
Icing (confectioner's) sugar	1 cup	250 mL
Quartered maraschino cherries, well-drained	1/2 cup	125 mL
Chopped walnuts	1/2 cup	125 mL
Large egg, fork-beaten	1	1
Medium unsweetened coconut	1/2 cup	125 mL

Heat chips and margarine in large heavy saucepan on lowest heat, stirring often, until chips are almost melted. Do not overheat. Remove from heat. Stir until smooth.

Add next 5 ingredients. Stir well. Let stand until cool enough to handle. Shape mixture into 2 1/2 inch (6.4 cm) diameter log.

Sprinkle coconut on waxed paper on work surface. Roll log in coconut until coated. Wrap in waxed paper or plastic wrap. Chill until firm. Cut into 1/2 inch (12 mm) slices, cleaning knife under hot water after each slice. Cuts into 24 slices.

1 slice: 116 Calories; 6.3 g Total Fat (1.9 g Mono, 1.2 g Poly, 2.8 g Sat); 9 mg Cholesterol; 16 g Carbohydrate; 1 g Fibre; 1 g Protein; 18 mg Sodium

Pictured on page 83.

A light, summer treat. Freezes well so you can pull one out whenever you get a craving.

Lemon Bars

BOTTOM LAYER

All-purpose flour	2 cups	500 mL
Icing (confectioner's) sugar	3/4 cup	175 mL
Hard margarine (or butter), softened, cut up	1 cup	250 mL

TOP LAYER

Large eggs	4	4
Lemon juice	1/3 cup	75 mL
Grated lemon peel	1 tbsp.	15 mL

(continued on next page)

Granulated sugar	1 1/2 cups	375 mL
All-purpose flour	1/4 cup	60 mL
Baking powder	1 tsp.	5 mL

Icing (confectioner's) sugar, for dusting

Bottom Layer: Combine flour and icing sugar in medium bowl. Cut in margarine until mixture resembles fine crumbs. Press firmly in ungreased 9 x 13 inch (22 x 33 cm) pan. Bake in 350°F (175°C) oven for about 20 minutes until golden. Remove from oven.

Top Layer: Beat eggs in large bowl until frothy. Add lemon juice and peel. Stir.

Combine granulated sugar, flour and baking powder in small bowl. Add to egg mixture. Stir until just moistened. Spread evenly over bottom layer. Bake for about 25 minutes until set. Let stand in pan on wire rack for 5 minutes.

Dust evenly with icing sugar using sieve. Let stand until cool. Cuts into 48 bars.

1 bar: 100 Calories; 4.5 g Total Fat (2.8 g Mono, 0.5 g Poly, 1 g Sat); 18 mg Cholesterol; 14 g Carbohydrate; trace Fibre; 1 g Protein; 60 mg Sodium

Pictured below.

Favourite date squares that are not as messy to eat as some others. These crumbs hold together well.

Matrimonial Squares

CRUMB LAYERS

Rolled oats (not instant)	1 1/2 cups	375 mL
All-purpose flour	1 1/4 cups	300 mL
Brown sugar, packed	1 cup	250 mL
Baking soda	1 tsp.	5 mL
Salt	1/2 tsp.	2 mL
Hard margarine (or butter), softened, cut up	1 cup	250 mL

DATE FILLING

Chopped pitted dates	1 1/2 cups	375 mL
Water	2/3 cup	150 mL
Granulated sugar	1/2 cup	125 mL

Crumb Layers: Combine first 5 ingredients in large bowl. Cut in margarine until mixture resembles very coarse crumbs. Press slightly more than 1/2 of mixture firmly in greased 9 x 9 inch (22 x 22 cm) pan. Set remaining mixture aside.

Date Filling: Combine dates, water and sugar in medium saucepan. Bring to a boil on medium. Reduce heat to medium-low. Simmer, uncovered, for about 10 minutes until dates are softened and water is almost evaporated, adding more water if necessary while simmering to soften dates. Spread evenly over bottom layer of crumbs. Sprinkle remaining crumb mixture evenly over top. Press down lightly. Bake in 350°F (175°C) oven for about 30 minutes until golden. Let stand in pan on wire rack until cool. Cuts into 36 squares.

1 square: 139 Calories; 5.7 g Total Fat (3.6 g Mono, 0.7 g Poly, 1.2 g Sat); 0 mg Cholesterol; 21 g Carbohydrate; 1 g Fibre; 1 g Protein; 134 mg Sodium

Pictured on page 87.

Top Right: Cherry Squares, page 88
Bottom Left: Matrimonial Squares, above

This is one of our most popular bar cookies. After you've tried a piece, you'll understand why.

Cherry Squares

BOTTOM LAYER

All-purpose flour	1 1/4 cups	300 mL
Brown sugar, packed	1/3 cup	75 mL
Hard margarine (or butter), softened, cut up	1/2 cup	125 mL

SECOND LAYER

Large eggs	2	2
Brown sugar, packed	1 1/4 cups	300 mL
All-purpose flour	1 tbsp.	15 mL
Baking powder	1/2 tsp.	2 mL
Salt	1/8 tsp.	0.5 mL
Medium unsweetened coconut	1 cup	250 mL
Chopped walnuts	1/2 cup	125 mL
Chopped red glazed cherries (or maraschino cherries, blotted dry)	1/2 cup	125 mL

VANILLA ICING

Icing (confectioner's) sugar	2 cups	500 mL
Hard margarine (or butter), softened	1/4 cup	60 mL
Milk (or water)	2 tbsp.	30 mL
Vanilla	1 tsp.	5 mL

Bottom Layer: Combine flour and brown sugar in small bowl. Cut in margarine until mixture resembles fine crumbs. Press firmly in ungreased 9 x 9 inch (22 x 22 cm) pan. Bake in 350°F (175°C) oven for 15 minutes. Remove from oven.

Second Layer: Beat eggs in medium bowl until frothy. Add remaining ingredients, in order given, stirring after each addition. Spread evenly over bottom layer. Bake for about 25 minutes until golden. Let stand in pan on wire rack until cooled completely.

Vanilla Icing: Beat all 4 ingredients in small bowl until smooth, adding more milk or icing sugar as necessary until spreading consistency. Spread evenly over second layer. Cuts into 36 squares.

1 square: 141 Calories; 6.4 g Total Fat (2.6 g Mono, 1.1 g Poly, 2.4 g Sat); 12 mg Cholesterol; 20 g Carbohydrate; trace Fibre; 2 g Protein; 62 mg Sodium

Pictured on page 87.

Apricot Zings

A long-time favourite. Great to make ahead and freeze. Perfect choice for a bake sale.

BOTTOM LAYER

Graham cracker crumbs	1 cup	250 mL
All-purpose flour	1 cup	250 mL
Brown sugar, packed	1 cup	250 mL
Hard margarine (or butter), melted	3/4 cup	175 mL
Medium unsweetened coconut	1/2 cup	125 mL
Salt	1/2 tsp.	2 mL

APRICOT FILLING

Dried apricots	1 cup	250 mL
Water		
Large eggs	2	2
Brown sugar, packed	1 cup	250 mL
Lemon juice	1 tbsp.	15 mL
All-purpose flour	1/3 cup	75 mL
Baking powder	1/2 tsp.	2 mL
Salt	1/4 tsp.	1 mL

Bottom Layer: Combine first 6 ingredients in medium bowl. Reserve 1 cup (250 mL) crumb mixture. Press remaining mixture firmly in ungreased 9 x 9 inch (22 x 22 cm) pan. Bake in 350°F (175°C) oven for 10 minutes. Remove from oven.

Apricot Filling: Place apricots in small saucepan. Add enough water to cover. Bring to a boil on medium. Reduce heat to medium-low. Simmer, uncovered, for about 15 minutes until apricots are softened. Drain well. Chop.

Beat eggs in medium bowl until frothy. Add brown sugar and lemon juice. Stir well.

Combine flour, baking powder and salt in small bowl. Add to egg mixture. Stir. Add apricots. Stir well. Spread evenly over bottom layer. Sprinkle with reserved crumbs. Bake for 30 to 35 minutes until golden. Let stand in pan on wire rack until cool. Cuts into 36 squares.

1 square: 135 Calories; 5.5 g Total Fat (2.9 g Mono, 0.5 g Poly, 1.7 g Sat); 12 mg Cholesterol; 21 g Carbohydrate; 1 g Fibre; 1 g Protein; 126 mg Sodium

Pictured on page 91.

Using soda crackers in this square gives it a bit of a different touch.

Lemon Crunch

BOTTOM LAYER

Crushed soda crackers	1 1/3 cups	325 mL
Hard margarine (or butter), softened	3/4 cup	175 mL
All-purpose flour	3/4 cup	175 mL
Granulated sugar	1/2 cup	125 mL
Medium unsweetened coconut	1/2 cup	125 mL
Baking powder	1 tsp.	5 mL

LEMON FILLING

Large eggs	3	3
Granulated sugar	1 cup	250 mL
Lemon, grated peel and juice	1	1
Hard margarine (or butter)	1/4 cup	60 mL

Bottom Layer: Combine all 6 ingredients in medium bowl until crumbly. Reserve 1 cup (250 mL) for topping. Press remaining crumb mixture firmly in ungreased 9 x 9 inch (22 x 22 cm) pan. Bake in 350°F (175°C) oven for 15 minutes. Remove from oven.

Lemon Filling: Beat eggs in heavy medium saucepan or top of double boiler. Add remaining 3 ingredients. Heat and stir on medium until thickened. Spread evenly over crumb layer in pan. Sprinkle reserved crumb mixture over top. Bake for about 20 minutes until golden brown. Let stand in pan on wire rack until cool. Cuts into 36 squares.

1 square: 122 Calories; 7.1 g Total Fat (3.9 g Mono, 0.7 g Poly, 2.1 g Sat); 18 mg Cholesterol; 14 g Carbohydrate; trace Fibre; 1 g Protein; 120 mg Sodium

Pictured on page 91.

Left: Apricot Zings, page 89
Right: Lemon Crunch, above

Tastes like a famous candy bar.

Candy Bar Squares

Semi-sweet chocolate chips	2 cups	500 mL
Peanut butter chips	1 cup	250 mL
Granulated sugar	1 1/4 cups	300 mL
Hard margarine (or butter)	1/3 cup	75 mL
Milk	1/3 cup	75 mL
Coarsely chopped salted peanuts	1/4 cup	60 mL
Smooth peanut butter	1/4 cup	60 mL
Marshmallow creme	1 cup	250 mL
Vanilla	1 tsp.	5 mL
Coarsely chopped salted peanuts	3/4 cup	175 mL
Caramels	40	40
Water	2 1/2 tbsp.	37 mL

Heat both chips in large heavy saucepan on lowest heat, stirring often, until chips are almost melted. Do not overheat. Remove from heat. Stir until smooth. Spread about 1/2 of mixture evenly in greased or foil-lined 9 x 13 inch (22 x 33 cm) pan. Let stand until firm.

Heat and stir sugar, margarine and milk in heavy medium saucepan on medium until boiling. Boil for 5 minutes, stirring often. Spread evenly over chip layer.

Sprinkle first amount of peanuts over top.

Heat and stir peanut butter in small heavy saucepan on lowest heat until melted. Remove from heat. Add marshmallow creme and vanilla. Stir until smooth. Spoon mixture in dabs, using 1 tsp. (5 mL) for each, over peanuts.

Sprinkle second amount of peanuts over top.

Heat and stir caramels and water in heavy medium saucepan on lowest heat until smooth. Spread evenly over peanuts. Reheat remaining 1/2 of chip mixture if necessary until spreading consistency. Spread evenly over caramel. Chill until firm. Cuts into 54 squares.

1 square: 139 Calories; 6.7 g Total Fat (2.8 g Mono, 1 g Poly, 2.6 g Sat); 0 mg Cholesterol; 20 g Carbohydrate; 1 g Fibre; 2 g Protein; 70 mg Sodium

Pictured on page 93 and on front cover.

When unexpected company calls, whip these up. They're ready in a flash—and will be eaten just as quickly.

Chocolate Cherry Slice

BOTTOM LAYER

Sweet chocolate baking squares (1 oz., 28 g, each), or 1 1/3 cups (325 mL) chocolate chips	8	8

TOP LAYER

Large eggs	2	2
Granulated sugar	1/2 cup	125 mL
Medium unsweetened coconut	1 1/2 cups	375 mL
Chopped glazed cherries	1/4 cup	60 mL

Icing (confectioner's) sugar, for dusting (optional)

Bottom Layer: Heat chocolate in small heavy saucepan on lowest heat, stirring often, until almost melted. Do not overheat. Remove from heat. Stir until smooth. Spread evenly in bottom of greased 8 x 8 inch (20 x 20 cm) pan. Chill until firm.

Top Layer: Beat eggs and sugar in medium bowl until thick and pale. Add coconut and cherries. Stir. Spread evenly over bottom layer. Bake in 350°F (175°C) oven for 25 to 30 minutes until golden and firm to the touch. Let stand in pan on wire rack until cool. Cover and store in refrigerator.

Just before serving, dust with icing sugar using a sieve. Cuts into 25 squares.

1 square: 112 Calories; 7.2 g Total Fat (1.3 g Mono, 0.2 g Poly, 5.2 g Sat); 17 mg Cholesterol; 13 g Carbohydrate; trace Fibre; 1 g Protein; 9 mg Sodium

Pictured on page 95.

1. Saucepan Brownies, page 97
2. Chocolate Cherry Slice, above
3. Cream Cheese Brownies, page 96

These are fussy to prepare, but are worth the extra time it takes. Very attractive.

variation

Omit the icing. They're delicious uniced.

Cream Cheese Brownies

CHEESE LAYER

Block of cream cheese, softened	4 oz.	125 g
Large egg	1	1
Granulated sugar	1/2 cup	125 mL
All-purpose flour	2 tbsp.	30 mL
Chopped maraschino cherries, well-drained	1/2 cup	125 mL

BROWNIE LAYER

Large eggs	2	2
Granulated sugar	1 cup	250 mL
All-purpose flour	3/4 cup	175 mL
Chopped walnuts	1/2 cup	125 mL
Salt	1/8 tsp.	0.5 mL
Hard margarine (or butter), cut up	1/2 cup	125 mL
Cocoa, sifted if lumpy	1/4 cup	60 mL

CHOCOLATE COFFEE ICING

Icing (confectioner's) sugar	1 1/3 cups	325 mL
Cocoa, sifted if lumpy	1/3 cup	75 mL
Hard margarine (or butter), softened	3 tbsp.	50 mL
Hot prepared strong coffee (or hot water)	1 1/2 tbsp.	25 mL

Cheese Layer: Beat cream cheese and egg in medium bowl until smooth. Combine sugar and flour in small bowl. Add to cream cheese mixture, 2 tbsp. (30 mL) at a time while beating, until smooth. Add cherries. Stir. Set aside.

Brownie Layer: Beat eggs in separate medium bowl until frothy. Add next 4 ingredients. Stir.

Heat and stir margarine and cocoa in small heavy saucepan on lowest heat until smooth. Add to egg mixture. Stir well. Spread about 2/3 of brownie mixture evenly in greased 9 x 9 inch (22 x 22 cm) pan. Spoon mounds of cream cheese mixture, using 1 tbsp. (15 mL) for each, over brownie layer. Spoon remaining brownie mixture in dabs, using 1/2 tsp. (2 mL) for each, over top. Mixtures will look patchy in pan. Bake in 350°F (175°C) oven for 30 to 35 minutes until edges pull away from sides of pan. Let stand in pan on wire rack until cooled completely.

(continued on next page)

Chocolate Coffee Icing: Beat all 4 ingredients in small bowl until smooth, adding more coffee or icing sugar as necessary until spreading consistency. Spread evenly over brownie layer. Cuts into 25 squares.

1 square: 189 Calories; 9.4 g Total Fat (4.6 g Mono, 1.7 g Poly, 2.6 g Sat); 31 mg Cholesterol; 25 g Carbohydrate; 1 g Fibre; 3 g Protein; 97 mg Sodium

Pictured on page 95.

Saucepan Brownies

A no-bake brownie with rich chocolate flavour.

Semi-sweet chocolate chips	2 2/3 cups	650 mL
Evaporated milk	1 cup	250 mL
Vanilla wafer crumbs	3 cups	750 mL
Miniature marshmallows	2 cups	500 mL
Chopped walnuts	1 cup	250 mL
Icing (confectioner's) sugar	1 cup	250 mL
Salt	1/2 tsp.	2 mL
Evaporated milk	2 tsp.	10 mL

Heat and stir chips and first amount of evaporated milk in large heavy saucepan on medium-low until smooth. Do not overheat. Remove from heat. Reserve 1/2 cup (125 mL) chocolate mixture. Set aside.

Add next 5 ingredients to remaining chocolate mixture. Stir well. Press firmly in greased or foil-lined 9 x 9 inch (22 x 22 cm) pan.

Add second amount of evaporated milk to reserved chocolate mixture. Stir well. Spread evenly over crumb mixture. Chill until firm. Cuts into 36 squares.

1 square: 149 Calories; 7.7 g Total Fat (2.4 g Mono, 1.8 g Poly, 3.1 g Sat); 6 mg Cholesterol; 20 g Carbohydrate; 1 g Fibre; 2 g Protein; 66 mg Sodium

Pictured on page 95.

These do melt in your mouth.

Chocolate Coconut Melts

Can of sweetened condensed milk	11 oz.	300 mL
Unsweetened chocolate baking squares (1 oz., 28 g, each), chopped	2	2
Salt	1/4 tsp.	1 mL
Flake coconut	2 2/3 cups	650 mL
Vanilla	1 tsp.	5 mL

Heat and stir condensed milk, chocolate and salt in heavy medium saucepan on medium-low until smooth. Remove from heat.

Add coconut and vanilla. Stir well. Spread evenly in greased 8 x 8 inch (20 x 20 cm) pan. Bake in 350°F (175°C) oven for about 20 minutes until set. Let stand in pan on wire rack until cool. Cuts into 25 squares.

1 square: 129 Calories; 9.1 g Total Fat (1.1 g Mono, 0.2 g Poly, 7.4 g Sat); 5 mg Cholesterol; 12 g Carbohydrate; 1 g Fibre; 2 g Protein; 48 mg Sodium

Pictured on page 99.

You'll need two pans to make these. Wrap individual bars in plastic wrap for an easy take-along breakfast when you roll out of bed and have to run out the door!

note

To toast seeds, place in single layer in ungreased shallow pan. Bake in 350°F (175°C) oven for 5 to 8 minutes, stirring or shaking often, until desired doneness.

Take-Along Breakfast Bars

Quick-cooking rolled oats (not instant)	4 cups	1 L
Medium unsweetened coconut	2 cups	500 mL
Lightly crushed cornflakes cereal	1 cup	250 mL
Chopped dried apricots	1 cup	250 mL
Raisins	1 cup	250 mL
Shelled sunflower seeds, toasted (see Note)	2/3 cup	150 mL
Hard margarine (or butter)	1/2 cup	125 mL
Can of sweetened condensed milk	11 oz.	300 mL
Golden corn syrup	1/4 cup	60 mL
Frozen concentrated orange juice	2 tbsp.	30 mL

(continued on next page)

Combine first 6 ingredients in large bowl.

Melt margarine in medium saucepan. Add remaining 3 ingredients. Heat and stir on low until smooth. Slowly pour into rolled oat mixture while stirring until well combined. Mixture will be sticky. Divide and press firmly in 2 greased 9 × 13 inch (22 × 33 cm) pans. Bake in 325°F (160°C) oven for 20 to 30 minutes until edges are golden. Let stand in pans on wire racks for 5 minutes. Score top of each into 2 × 3 inch (5 × 7.5 cm) bars with knife. Let stand until cool. Each pan cuts into 18 bars, for a total of 36 bars.

1 bar: 197 Calories; 9.4 g Total Fat (2.7 g Mono, 1.6 g Poly, 4.5 g Sat); 4 mg Cholesterol; 26 g Carbohydrate; 2 g Fibre; 4 g Protein; 79 mg Sodium

Pictured below.

Top: Take-Along Breakfast Bars, page 98
Bottom: Chocolate Coconut Melts, page 98

take-along breakfast cookies

Roll out mixture between 2 sheets of greased waxed paper to 1/2 inch (12 mm) thickness. Cut into shapes with cookie cutter. Carefully transfer to greased cookie sheets. Bake in 325°F (160°C) oven for 15 to 20 minutes until edges are golden. Let stand on sheets for 5 minutes before removing to wire racks to cool. Makes about 24 cookies.

Brittle lovers take note: lots of peanuts covered in chocolate. A dream come true!

Chocolate Brittle

Granulated sugar	1 cup	250 mL
White corn syrup	1/2 cup	125 mL
Roasted salted peanuts	1 cup	250 mL
Hard margarine (or butter)	2 tbsp.	30 mL
Vanilla	1 tsp.	5 mL
Baking soda	1 1/2 tsp.	7 mL
TOPPING		
Semi-sweet chocolate chips	3/4 cup	175 mL
Chopped unsalted peanuts	1/3 cup	75 mL

Combine sugar and corn syrup in ungreased 2 quart (2 L) casserole. Microwave, uncovered, on high (100%) for about 4 minutes until sugar is dissolved and mixture is bubbling.

Add peanuts. Stir. Microwave, uncovered, on high (100%) for about 6 minutes, checking at 1 minute intervals, until golden.

Add margarine and vanilla. Stir. Microwave, uncovered, on high (100%) for 1 minute. Stir.

Add baking soda. Stir. Mixture will foam. Immediately turn out onto greased baking sheet with sides. Spread evenly into thin layer.

Topping: Sprinkle chips over hot peanut mixture. Let stand until chips are softened. Spread evenly. Sprinkle with chopped peanuts. Chill until set. Break into irregular-shaped pieces, about 1 1/2 x 2 inches (3.8 x 5 cm) each. Makes about 1 1/4 lbs. (560 g), or about 30 pieces.

1 piece: *114 Calories; 5.5 g Total Fat (2.6 g Mono, 1.2 g Poly, 1.4 g Sat); 0 mg Cholesterol; 16 g Carbohydrate; 1 g Fibre; 2 g Protein; 120 mg Sodium*

Pictured on page 101.

Top Left: Chocolate Nuts, page 102
Top Right: Chocolate Marshmallows, page 102
Bottom: Chocolate Brittle, above

These are a pleasant change from the usual mixed nut offering.

Chocolate Nuts

Pecan halves	1 cup	250 mL
Walnut halves	1 cup	250 mL
Chocolate syrup	1/2 cup	125 mL
Cooking oil	4 tsp.	20 mL

Measure pecans and walnuts into medium bowl. Add chocolate syrup and cooking oil. Stir until nuts are well coated. Spread evenly in greased baking sheet with sides. Bake in 350ºF (175ºC) oven for 8 to 10 minutes, stirring halfway through baking time, until dry and crisp. Makes 2 cups (500 mL).

2 tbsp. (30 mL): 117 Calories; 9.7 g Total Fat (4.5 g Mono, 4 g Poly, 0.9 g Sat); 0 mg Cholesterol; 8 g Carbohydrate; 1 g Fibre; 2 g Protein; 10 mg Sodium

Pictured on page 101.

Allow extra time for this impressive-looking candy dessert. Certainly worth the effort.

note

To toast nuts, place in single layer in ungreased shallow pan. Bake in 350ºF (175ºC) oven for 5 to 8 minutes, stirring or shaking often, until desired doneness.

Chocolate Marshmallows

Can of sweetened condensed milk	11 oz.	300 mL
Jar of marshmallow creme	7 oz.	198 g
Semi-sweet chocolate chips	2 1/3 cups	575 mL
Large marshmallows	60	60
Finely chopped walnuts (or pecans), toasted (see Note)	4 1/2 cups	1.1 L

Heat and stir condensed milk, marshmallow creme and chips in medium saucepan on low until smooth. Remove from heat.

Roll 1 marshmallow in chocolate mixture until coated using fork, allowing excess chocolate to drip back into saucepan. Roll in chopped walnuts in small bowl until coated. Place on waxed paper-lined baking sheet. Repeat with remaining marshmallows, chocolate mixture and walnuts. If chocolate mixture becomes too thick for dipping, reheat on low until desired consistency. Let marshmallows stand overnight until set. Makes 60 chocolate marshmallows.

1 chocolate marshmallow: 147 Calories; 8.3 g Total Fat (2.1 g Mono, 3.8 g Poly, 1.9 g Sat); 2 mg Cholesterol; 18 g Carbohydrate; 1 g Fibre; 3 g Protein; 14 mg Sodium

Pictured on page 101.

Cranberry Almond Bark

White chocolate bars (3 1/2 oz., 100 g, each), chopped	5	5
Whole almonds (with skin)	1 1/2 cups	375 mL
Dried cranberries	1 cup	250 mL

Homemade chocolate bark may not be much less expensive than store-bought, but it tastes so much better!

Heat chocolate in heavy medium saucepan on lowest heat, stirring often, until chocolate is almost melted. Do not overheat. Remove from heat. Stir until smooth.

Add almonds and cranberries. Stir until well coated. Spread on waxed paper-lined baking sheet with sides to 1/4 inch (6 mm) thickness. Chill until set. Break into irregular-shaped pieces, about 1 1/2 × 2 inches (3.8 × 5 cm) each. Makes about 56 pieces.

1 piece: 75 Calories; 4.8 g Total Fat (2.2 g Mono, 0.5 g Poly, 1.8 g Sat); 2 mg Cholesterol; 7 g Carbohydrate; 1 g Fibre; 1 g Protein; 8 mg Sodium

Pictured below.

Whether they've been naughty or nice, your guests deserve these melt-in-your-mouth truffles.

Apricot Brandy Truffles

Whipping cream	1/4 cup	60 mL
Butter (not margarine)	2 tbsp.	30 mL
White chocolate bars (3 1/2 oz., 100 g, each), finely chopped	3	3
Finely chopped dried apricots	3/4 cup	175 mL
Brandy (or 1 tsp., 5 mL, brandy flavouring)	1 tbsp.	15 mL
White chocolate melting wafers	1 cup	250 mL
Medium unsweetened coconut	1/4 cup	60 mL
Dark chocolate melting wafers	1 cup	250 mL

Heat and stir whipping cream and butter in small heavy saucepan on medium-high until boiling. Immediately remove from heat. Add chocolate bar pieces. Stir until chocolate is melted. Transfer to medium bowl.

Add apricot and brandy. Stir well. Chill, uncovered, for about 50 minutes, stirring twice, until just firm but not set. Roll into 25 balls, using 1 tbsp. (15 mL) for each. Chill for 30 minutes.

Heat white chocolate wafers in small heavy saucepan on lowest heat, stirring often, until almost melted. Do not overheat. Remove from heat. Stir until smooth. Dip 12 balls into white chocolate using fork, allowing excess to drip back into saucepan. Roll in coconut in small bowl. Place on waxed paper-lined baking sheet. If chocolate becomes too thick for dipping, reheat on low until desired consistency.

Heat dark chocolate wafers in separate small heavy saucepan on lowest heat, stirring often, until almost melted. Do not overheat. Remove from heat. Stir until smooth. Dip remaining balls into dark chocolate using fork, allowing excess to drip back into saucepan. Place on same baking sheet. If chocolate becomes too thick for dipping, reheat on low until desired consistency. Chill for about 30 minutes until set. Makes 25 truffles.

1 truffle: 168 Calories; 10.3 g Total Fat (3.1 g Mono, 0.3 g Poly, 6.3 g Sat); 10 mg Cholesterol; 19 g Carbohydrate; 1 g Fibre; 2 g Protein; 29 mg Sodium

Pictured on page 105.

Top: Rum Balls, page 106
Bottom: Apricot Brandy Truffles, above

A classic sweet for Christmas gift-giving.

Rum Balls

Chocolate cake mix (1 layer size)	1	1
Brown sugar, packed	1/4 cup	60 mL
Cocoa, sifted if lumpy	2 tbsp.	30 mL
Apricot jam	1/4 cup	60 mL
Dark (navy) rum	2 tbsp.	30 mL
Boiling water	1 tbsp.	15 mL
Chocolate sprinkles	1/2 – 3/4 cup	125 – 175 mL

Prepare and bake cake mix according to package directions. Let stand in pan on wire rack until cooled completely. Partially freeze. Crumble into large bowl.

Add brown sugar and cocoa. Stir.

Combine jam, rum and boiling water in small cup. Add to cake crumbs. Stir well. Shape into balls, using 1 1/2 tbsp. (25 mL) crumb mixture for each.

Roll each ball in chocolate sprinkles in small bowl. Chill. Makes 24 rum balls.

1 rum ball: 74 Calories; 1.8 g Total Fat (0.8 g Mono, 0.1 g Poly, 0.9 g Sat); 1 mg Cholesterol; 14 g Carbohydrate; trace Fibre; 1 g Protein; 89 mg Sodium

Pictured on page 105.

So pretty and such a sweet treat!

Pinwheels

Icing (confectioner's) sugar	2 1/2 cups	625 mL
Mashed potatoes	1/3 cup	75 mL
Vanilla	1/2 tsp.	2 mL
Salt	1/8 tsp.	0.5 mL
Icing (confectioner's) sugar, for dusting		
Smooth peanut butter	1/3 cup	75 mL

Combine first 4 ingredients in large bowl.

(continued on next page)

Turn out onto work surface dusted with icing sugar. Knead until smooth, adding more icing sugar if necessary, until a pliable but not sticky dough forms. Divide into 3 equal portions. Roll out 1 portion on surface dusted with icing sugar to 5 x 8 inch (12.5 x 20 cm) rectangle, 1/8 inch (3 mm) thick.

Spread about 1 1/2 tbsp. (25 mL) peanut butter evenly over top. Roll up, jelly roll-style, from long side. Wrap with plastic wrap. Chill. Repeat with remaining portions. Cut each roll into 1/4 inch (6 mm) slices. Makes about 6 dozen (72) pinwheels.

1 pinwheel: 25 Calories; 0.7 g Total Fat (0.3 g Mono, 0.2 g Poly, 0.1 g Sat); 0 mg Cholesterol; 5 g Carbohydrate; trace Fibre; 0 g Protein; 13 mg Sodium

Pictured below.

This is a soft, creamy fudge, so place in a sturdy container for gift-giving. A perfect blend of chocolate and peanuts.

note

To toast nuts, place in single layer in ungreased shallow pan. Bake in 350°F (175°C) oven for 5 to 8 minutes, stirring or shaking often, until desired doneness.

Choco-Peanut Fudge

Granulated sugar	2 cups	500 mL
Cocoa, sifted if lumpy	1/3 cup	75 mL
Milk	3/4 cup	175 mL
Golden corn syrup	2 tbsp.	30 mL
Hard margarine (or butter)	2 tbsp.	30 mL
Salt	1/8 tsp.	0.5 mL
Smooth peanut butter	1/3 cup	75 mL
Chopped unsalted peanuts (or walnuts), toasted (see Note)	1/2 cup	125 mL

Combine first 6 ingredients in large heavy saucepan. Bring to a boil on medium, stirring constantly. Reduce heat to medium-low. Brush side of saucepan with damp pastry brush to dissolve any sugar crystals. Simmer, uncovered, for about 30 minutes, without stirring, until mixture reaches soft ball stage: 234 to 240°F (112 to 116°C) on candy thermometer or until about 1/4 tsp. (1 mL) of mixture dropped into very cold water forms a soft ball that flattens on its own when removed. Let stand, without stirring, until bottom of saucepan is cool enough to touch.

Add peanut butter and peanuts. Beat with spoon until mixture loses its shine and pulls away from side of saucepan. Spread evenly in greased 8 x 8 inch (20 x 20 cm) pan. Chill until firm. Makes 1 1/2 lbs. (680 g) fudge. Cuts into 36 pieces.

1 piece: 86 Calories; 3.2 g Total Fat (1.6 g Mono, 0.8 g Poly, 0.6 g Sat); 0 mg Cholesterol; 14 g Carbohydrate; 1 g Fibre; 1 g Protein; 32 mg Sodium

Pictured on page 109.

Marshmallow creme adds a definite creaminess to this rich, sweet fudge.

White Creme Fudge

Granulated sugar	2 cups	500 mL
Half-and-half cream	2/3 cup	150 mL
Hard margarine (or butter)	1/4 cup	60 mL
White corn syrup	1 tbsp.	15 mL
White chocolate baking squares (1 oz., 28 g, each), chopped	8	8
Jar of marshmallow creme	7 oz.	198 g

(continued on next page)

Quartered glazed cherries	1/4 cup	60 mL

Heat and stir first 4 ingredients in large heavy saucepan on medium-low until boiling. Brush side of saucepan with damp pastry brush to dissolve any sugar crystals. Boil for about 30 minutes, without stirring, until mixture reaches soft ball stage: 234 to 240°F (112 to 116°C) on candy thermometer or until about 1/4 tsp. (1 mL) of mixture dropped into very cold water forms a soft ball that flattens on its own when removed. Remove from heat.

Add chocolate and marshmallow creme. Stir until chocolate is melted and mixture is smooth.

Add cherries. Stir. Spread evenly in greased 8 × 8 inch (20 × 20 cm) pan. Chill until firm. Makes about 2 lbs. (900 g) fudge. Cuts into 36 pieces.

1 piece: 120 Calories; 3.7 g Total Fat (1.6 g Mono, 0.2 g Poly, 1.7 g Sat); 3 mg Cholesterol; 22 g Carbohydrate; trace Fibre; 1 g Protein; 26 mg Sodium

Pictured below.

Inner Circle: White Creme Fudge, page 108
Outer Circle: Choco-Peanut Fudge, page 108

The ultimate snack for those who love white chocolate and caramel corn. The perfect pick-me-up.

note

To toast nuts, place in single layer in ungreased shallow pan. Bake in 350°F (175°C) oven for 5 to 8 minutes, stirring or shaking often, until desired doneness.

These take extra time, but are fun to make. Freeze in an airtight container.

White Chocolate Popcorn

White chocolate bars (3 1/2 oz., 100 g, each), chopped	3	3
Bag of caramel-coated popcorn and peanuts (about 5 cups, 1.25 L)	7 oz.	200 g
Slivered almonds, toasted (see Note)	1/2 cup	125 mL

Heat chocolate in heavy medium saucepan on lowest heat, stirring often, until chocolate is almost melted. Do not overheat. Remove from heat. Stir until smooth.

Spread popcorn on foil-lined baking sheet with sides. Drizzle chocolate over popcorn. Stir. Sprinkle with almonds. Chill until set. Break into bite-size pieces. Makes about 5 1/2 cups (1.4 L).

1/2 cup (125 mL): 255 Calories; 13 g Total Fat (5.2 g Mono, 1.5 g Poly, 5.3 g Sat); 6 mg Cholesterol; 33 g Carbohydrate; 1 g Fibre; 4 g Protein; 79 mg Sodium

Pictured on page 111.

Marshmallow Delights

Butterscotch toffee bars (such as Mackintosh's), 2 oz. (56 g) each, broken up	3	3
Sweetened condensed milk	2/3 cup	150 mL
Hard margarine (or butter)	1/4 cup	60 mL
Large marshmallows	30	30
Special K cereal	4 cups	1 L

Heat and stir toffee, condensed milk and margarine in small heavy saucepan on medium until toffee is melted and mixture is smooth. Remove from heat.

Dip 1 marshmallow in toffee mixture until coated using fork. If toffee mixture becomes too thick for dipping, reheat on medium until desired consistency.

(continued on next page)

Roll coated marshmallow in cereal in medium bowl until coated using fork.
Place on waxed paper-lined baking sheet. Repeat with remaining marshmallows,
toffee mixture and cereal. Let marshmallows stand until set. Makes 30.

1 marshmallow delight: 95 Calories; 2.5 g Total Fat (1.3 g Mono, 0.2 g Poly, 0.8 g Sat); 3 mg Cholesterol;
18 g Carbohydrate; trace Fibre; 1 g Protein; 63 mg Sodium

Pictured below.

Top Left: Marshmallow Delights, page 110
Top Right: White Chocolate Popcorn,
    page 110
Bottom: Crispy Roll, page 112

Crisp cereal roll with a yummy chocolate filling.

Crispy Roll

White corn syrup	1 cup	250 mL
Smooth peanut butter	1 cup	250 mL
Granulated sugar	1 cup	250 mL
Hard margarine (or butter)	3 tbsp.	50 mL
Crisp rice cereal	6 cups	1.5 L

FILLING

Icing (confectioner's) sugar	2 cups	500 mL
Cocoa, sifted if lumpy	1 cup	250 mL
Hard margarine (or butter), softened	1/2 cup	125 mL
Water	1/4 cup	60 mL
Vanilla	1 tsp.	5 mL

Heat and stir first 4 ingredients in large heavy saucepan on medium-high until boiling. Immediately remove from heat.

Add cereal. Stir until coated. Place sheet of waxed paper on damp work surface so paper will stay in place. Turn out cereal mixture onto waxed paper. Press into 10 x 15 inch (25 x 38 cm) rectangle. Let stand for 15 to 20 minutes until set, but still warm.

Filling: Beat all 5 ingredients on low in large bowl until combined. Beat on medium until smooth, adding more water if necessary until spreading consistency. Spread evenly over cereal mixture. Roll up, jelly roll-style, from long side, using waxed paper as guide. Wrap in plastic wrap. Chill. Cuts into 24 slices.

1 slice: 273 Calories; 11.8 g Total Fat (6.5 g Mono, 2.1 g Poly, 2.6 g Sat); 0 mg Cholesterol; 41 g Carbohydrate; 2 g Fibre; 4 g Protein; 202 mg Sodium

Pictured on page 111.

Frozen Cheesecake Bites

A creamy lemon cheesecake on a buttery shortbread base. Almonds add a crunch.

BOTTOM LAYER

All-purpose flour	1 1/2 cups	375 mL
Icing (confectioner's) sugar	2 tbsp.	30 mL
Sliced almonds	3/4 cup	175 mL
Hard margarine (or butter), softened, cut up	1/2 cup	125 mL

TOP LAYER

Blocks of cream cheese (8 oz., 250 g, each), softened	2	2
Container of lemon yogurt	6 oz.	175 mL
Large eggs	2	2
Granulated sugar	1/2 cup	125 mL
Cream of wheat (unprepared)	2 tbsp.	30 mL
Finely grated lemon zest	1 tbsp.	15 mL
Vanilla	1/2 tsp.	2 mL
Sliced almonds (optional)	1/4 cup	60 mL

Bottom Layer: Combine first 3 ingredients in medium bowl. Cut in margarine until mixture resembles coarse crumbs. Press firmly in greased 9 × 13 inch (22 × 33 cm) pan. Bake in 350°F (175°C) oven for 10 minutes. Let stand in pan on wire rack for 5 minutes.

Top Layer: Beat first 7 ingredients in medium bowl until smooth. Spread evenly over bottom layer.

Sprinkle second amount of almonds over top. Bake for 25 to 30 minutes until set and edges are golden. Let stand in pan on wire rack until cooled completely. Cut into 15 rectangles with a wet knife. Cut each rectangle diagonally to make 2 triangles, for a total of 30 triangles. Arrange triangles 1/2 inch (12 mm) apart on ungreased baking sheet. Freeze for 2 to 3 hours until firm. Store in resealable freezer bags or tins, separating layers with waxed paper. Freeze until ready to serve. Makes 30.

1 cheesecake bite: 157 Calories; 11 g Total Fat (4.9 g Mono, 0.9 g Poly, 4.6 g Sat); 33 mg Cholesterol; 12 g Carbohydrate; 1 g Fibre; 3 g Protein; 95 mg Sodium

Pictured on page 115.

Photo Legend next page
1. Chipper Muffins, page 116
2. Butterscotch Muffins, page 116
3. Lemon Loaf, page 117
4. Frozen Cheesecake Bites, this page

Butterscotch Muffins

Hard margarine (or butter), softened	6 tbsp.	100 mL
Brown sugar, packed	1/4 cup	60 mL
Large egg	1	1
Milk	1 1/4 cups	300 mL
All-purpose flour	2 cups	500 mL
Box of instant butterscotch pudding powder (4 serving size)	4 oz.	113 g
Butterscotch chips	2/3 cup	150 mL
Baking powder	1 tbsp.	15 mL
Salt	1/2 tsp.	2 mL

Beat margarine and brown sugar in large bowl until light and creamy. Add egg. Beat. Add milk. Beat well.

Combine remaining 5 ingredients in medium bowl. Make a well in centre. Add margarine mixture to well. Stir until just moistened. Grease 12 muffin cups with cooking spray. Fill cups 3/4 full. Bake in 400°F (205°C) oven for about 18 minutes until golden, and wooden pick inserted in centre of muffin comes out clean. Let stand in pan for 5 minutes before removing to wire rack to cool. Makes 12 muffins.

1 muffin: 231 Calories; 7.2 g Total Fat (4.1 g Mono, 0.8 g Poly, 1.7 g Sat); 20 mg Cholesterol; 39 g Carbohydrate; 1 g Fibre; 4 g Protein; 405 mg Sodium

Pictured on page 114.

Chipper Muffins

All-purpose flour	1 3/4 cups	425 mL
Semi-sweet chocolate chips	1 cup	250 mL
Granulated sugar	3/4 cup	175 mL
Cocoa, sifted if lumpy	1/3 cup	75 mL
Baking powder	1 tbsp.	15 mL
Salt	1/2 tsp.	2 mL
Large egg	1	1
Milk	1 cup	250 mL
Cooking oil	1/3 cup	75 mL
Vanilla	1 tsp.	5 mL

(continued on next page)

Combine first 6 ingredients in medium bowl. Make a well in centre.

Beat egg in small bowl. Add milk, cooking oil and vanilla. Stir. Pour into well. Stir until just moistened. Grease 12 muffin cups with cooking spray. Fill cups 3/4 full. Bake in 400°F (205°C) oven for about 20 minutes until golden, and wooden pick inserted in centre of muffin comes out clean. Let stand in pan for 5 minutes before removing to wire rack to cool. Makes 12 muffins.

1 muffin: 271 Calories; 12 g Total Fat (5.6 g Mono, 2.2 g Poly, 3.6 g Sat); 19 mg Cholesterol; 40 g Carbohydrate; 2 g Fibre; 4 g Protein; 210 mg Sodium

Pictured on page 114.

Lemon Loaf

Hard margarine (or butter), softened	1/2 cup	125 mL
Granulated sugar	1 cup	250 mL
Large eggs	2	2
Milk	1/2 cup	125 mL
All-purpose flour	1 1/2 cups	375 mL
Grated lemon peel	1 tbsp.	15 mL
Baking powder	1 tsp.	5 mL
Salt	1/2 tsp.	2 mL
LEMON GLAZE		
Lemon juice	1/3 cup	75 mL
Granulated sugar	1/4 cup	60 mL

The glaze completes the delightful flavour of this loaf.

Cream margarine and sugar in large bowl. Add eggs, 1 at a time, beating well after each addition. Add milk. Beat well.

Combine next 4 ingredients in small bowl. Add to margarine mixture. Stir until just moistened. Spread evenly in greased 9 x 5 x 3 inch (22 x 12.5 x 7.5 cm) loaf pan. Bake in 350°F (175°C) oven for about 60 minutes until wooden pick inserted in centre comes out clean.

Lemon Glaze: Heat and stir lemon juice and sugar in small saucepan on medium until sugar is dissolved. Spoon evenly over top of hot loaf. Let stand for 10 minutes before removing from pan to wire rack to cool. Cuts into 16 slices.

1 slice: 177 Calories; 6.9 g Total Fat (4.2 g Mono, 0.7 g Poly, 1.5 g Sat); 27 mg Cholesterol; 27 g Carbohydrate; trace Fibre; 2 g Protein; 180 mg Sodium

Pictured on page 115.

A tender loaf with a delicate apple flavour.

note

To toast nuts, place in single layer in ungreased shallow pan. Bake in 350°F (175°C) oven for 5 to 8 minutes, stirring or shaking often, until desired doneness.

Apple Loaf

Hard margarine (or butter), softened	1/2 cup	125 mL
Granulated sugar	1 cup	250 mL
Large eggs	2	2
Milk	1/3 cup	75 mL
Vanilla	1 tsp.	5 mL
Coarsely grated, tart cooking apple (such as Granny Smith), with peel, packed	1 cup	250 mL
All-purpose flour	2 cups	500 mL
Baking powder	1 tsp.	5 mL
Baking soda	1/2 tsp.	2 mL
Salt	1/2 tsp.	2 mL
Chopped walnuts, toasted (see Note)	1/2 cup	125 mL

Cream margarine and sugar in large bowl. Add eggs, 1 at a time, beating well after each addition. Add milk and vanilla. Beat.

Add apple. Stir.

Combine remaining 5 ingredients in medium bowl. Add to apple mixture. Stir until just moistened. Spread evenly in greased 9 x 5 x 3 inch (22 x 12.5 x 7.5 cm) loaf pan. Bake in 350°F (175°C) oven for about 60 minutes until wooden pick inserted in centre comes out clean. Let stand in pan for 10 minutes before removing to wire rack to cool. Cuts into 16 slices.

1 slice: 207 Calories; 9.2 g Total Fat (4.7 g Mono, 2.3 g Poly, 1.7 g Sat); 27 mg Cholesterol; 28 g Carbohydrate; 1 g Fibre; 4 g Protein; 219 mg Sodium

Pictured on page 119.

Comfort is sitting down and enjoying this muffin with a cup of your favourite hot beverage. Great served any time.

Apple Streusel Muffins

TOPPING

Brown sugar, packed	1/4 cup	60 mL
All-purpose flour	2 tbsp.	30 mL
Ground cinnamon	1/8 tsp.	0.5 mL
Hard margarine (or butter), softened	1 tbsp.	15 mL
All-purpose flour	1 1/2 cups	375 mL
Granulated sugar	1/2 cup	125 mL
Baking powder	1 tbsp.	15 mL
Salt	1/2 tsp.	2 mL
Large egg	1	1
Milk	2/3 cup	150 mL
Cooking oil	1/4 cup	60 mL
Peeled, shredded cooking apple (such as McIntosh), packed	3/4 cup	175 mL

Topping: Combine brown sugar, flour and cinnamon in small bowl. Cut in margarine until mixture resembles coarse crumbs. Set aside.

Combine next 4 ingredients in large bowl. Make a well in centre.

Beat egg, milk and cooking oil in small bowl. Add apple. Stir. Pour into well. Stir until just moistened. Grease 12 muffin cups with cooking spray. Fill cups 3/4 full. Divide and sprinkle topping over each. Bake in 400°F (205°C) oven for 15 to 20 minutes until golden, and wooden pick inserted in centre of muffin comes out clean. Let stand in pan for 5 minutes before removing to wire rack to cool. Makes 12 muffins.

1 muffin: 196 Calories; 6.6 g Total Fat (3.7 g Mono, 1.7 g Poly, 0.4 g Sat); 19 mg Cholesterol; 29 g Carbohydrate; 1 g Fibre; 3 g Protein; 218 mg Sodium

Pictured on page 121.

Small melt-in-your-mouth mints. Cutting them with scissors gives them a pretty look.

After-Dinner Mints

Envelopes of unflavoured gelatin (1 tbsp., 15 mL, each)	3	3
Cold water	1/2 cup	125 mL
Icing (confectioner's) sugar	2 cups	500 mL
Peppermint flavouring	1 1/2 tsp.	7 mL
Baking powder	1/4 tsp.	1 mL
Icing (confectioner's) sugar	4 cups	1 L

Sprinkle gelatin over water in medium saucepan. Let stand for 1 minute. Heat and stir on low until gelatin is dissolved. Remove from heat.

Add first amount of icing sugar, peppermint flavouring and baking powder. Stir well.

Add second amount of icing sugar. Stir. Mixture will be sticky. Turn out onto work surface dusted with icing sugar. Knead dough for about 1 minute until smooth. Divide into 4 equal portions. Cover 3 portions with plastic wrap to prevent drying. Roll out 1 portion into 1/2 inch (12 mm) diameter rope. Slice into 1/2 inch (12 mm) pieces with scissors or knife. Arrange in single layer on waxed paper-lined baking sheet. Repeat with remaining portions. Let stand for about 1 hour until firm. Store in resealable plastic bags. Makes about 168 mints.

1 mint: 18 Calories; 0 g Total Fat (0 g Mono, 0 g Poly, 0 g Sat); 0 mg Cholesterol; 5 g Carbohydrate; 0 g Fibre; 0 g Protein; 1 mg Sodium

Pictured on page 123.

An all-chocolate, creamy, don't-have-to-wait-until-after-eight mint.

note

A few more drops of flavouring may be added to dough to increase mint flavour.

Fudgy Chocolate Mints

Semi-sweet chocolate chips	2 cups	500 mL
Can of sweetened condensed milk	11 oz.	300 mL
Milk chocolate chips	1 cup	250 mL
Hard margarine (or butter)	2 tbsp.	30 mL
Vanilla	1 tsp.	5 mL
Peppermint flavouring (see Note)	1/8 tsp.	0.5 mL

(continued on next page)

Heat and stir all 6 ingredients in large heavy saucepan on medium-low until chocolate is melted and mixture is smooth. Spread evenly in greased or foil-lined 9 × 9 inch (22 × 22 cm) pan. Let stand until set. Cut into 12 rows lengthwise and crosswise, for a total of 144 mints.

1 mint: 28 Calories; 1.5 g Total Fat (0.5 g Mono, 0.1 g Poly, 0.9 g Sat); 1 mg Cholesterol; 4 g Carbohydrate; trace Fibre; 0 g Protein; 7 mg Sodium

Pictured below.

variation

For small candies, drop, using 2 tsp. (10 mL) for each, onto waxed paper. Let stand until set. If chocolate mixture becomes too hard to drop, reheat on low until desired consistency.

Left: Fudgy Chocolate Mints, page 122
Right: After-Dinner Mints, page 122

Throughout this book measurements are given in Conventional and Metric measure. To compensate for differences between the two measurements due to rounding, a full metric measure is not always used. The cup used is the standard 8 fluid ounce. Temperature is given in degrees Fahrenheit and Celsius. Baking pan measurements are in inches and centimetres as well as quarts and litres. An exact metric conversion is given on this page as well as the working equivalent (Metric Standard Measure).

Pans

Conventional – Inches	Metric – Centimetres
8 x 8 inch	20 x 20 cm
9 x 9 inch	22 x 22 cm
9 x 13 inch	22 x 33 cm
10 x 15 inch	25 x 38 cm
11 x 17 inch	28 x 43 cm
8 x 2 inch round	20 x 5 cm
9 x 2 inch round	22 x 5 cm
10 x 4 1/2 inch tube	25 x 11 cm
8 x 4 x 3 inch loaf	20 x 10 x 7.5 cm
9 x 5 x 3 inch loaf	22 x 12.5 x 7.5 cm

Oven Temperatures

Fahrenheit (°F)	Celsius (°C)	Fahrenheit (°F)	Celsius (°C)
175°	80°	350°	175°
200°	95°	375°	190°
225°	110°	400°	205°
250°	120°	425°	220°
275°	140°	450°	230°
300°	150°	475°	240°
325°	160°	500°	260°

Spoons

Conventional Measure	Metric Exact Conversion Millilitre (mL)	Metric Standard Measure Millilitre (mL)
1/8 teaspoon (tsp.)	0.6 mL	0.5 mL
1/4 teaspoon (tsp.)	1.2 mL	1 mL
1/2 teaspoon (tsp.)	2.4 mL	2 mL
1 teaspoon (tsp.)	4.7 mL	5 mL
2 teaspoons (tsp.)	9.4 mL	10 mL
1 tablespoon (tbsp.)	14.2 mL	15 mL

Cups

1/4 cup (4 tbsp.)	56.8 mL	60 mL
1/3 cup (5 1/3 tbsp.)	75.6 mL	75 mL
1/2 cup (8 tbsp.)	113.7 mL	125 mL
2/3 cup (10 2/3 tbsp.)	151.2 mL	150 mL
3/4 cup (12 tbsp.)	170.5 mL	175 mL
1 cup (16 tbsp.)	227.3 mL	250 mL
4 1/2 cups	1022.9 mL	1000 mL(1 L)

Dry Measurements

Conventional Measure Ounces (oz.)	Metric Exact Conversion Grams (g)	Metric Standard Measure Grams (g)
1 oz.	28.3 g	28 g
2 oz.	56.7 g	57 g
3 oz.	85.0 g	85 g
4 oz.	113.4 g	125 g
5 oz.	141.7 g	140 g
6 oz.	170.1 g	170 g
7 oz.	198.4 g	200 g
8 oz.	226.8 g	250 g
16 oz.	453.6 g	500 g
32 oz.	907.2 g	1000 g (1 kg)

Casseroles

Canada & Britain		United States	
Standard Size Casserole	Exact Metric Measure	Standard Size Casserole	Exact Metric Measure
1 qt. (5 cups)	1.13 L	1 qt. (4 cups)	900 mL
1 1/2 qts. (7 1/2 cups)	1.69 L	1 1/2 qts. (6 cups)	1.35 L
2 qts. (10 cups)	2.25 L	2 qts. (8 cups)	1.8 L
2 1/2 qts. (12 1/2 cups)	2.81 L	2 1/2 qts. (10 cups)	2.25 L
3 qts. (15 cups)	3.38 L	3 qts. (12 cups)	2.7 L
4 qts. (20 cups)	4.5 L	4 qts. (16 cups)	3.6 L
5 qts. (25 cups)	5.63 L	5 qts. (20 cups)	4.5 L

most loved

Company's Coming

Cookies

most loved recipe collection by Jean Paré

most loved

Cookies

Pictured on divider:
Decadent Chocolate Chippers, page 16

We gratefully acknowledge the following
suppliers for their generous support of our
Test and Photography Kitchens:

Corelle®
Hamilton Beach® Canada
Lagostina®
Proctor Silex® Canada
Tupperware®

Our special thanks to the following
businesses for providing extensive props
for photography:

A Taste of Provence
Anchor Hocking Canada
Browne & Co.
Canhome Global
Casa Bugatti
Cherison Enterprises Inc.
Corelle®
Danesco Inc.
Emile Henry
Island Pottery Inc.
Klass Works
La Cache
Linens 'N Things
Mikasa Home Store
Out of the Fire Studio
Pfaltzgraff Canada
Pier 1 Imports
Stokes

Pictured from left: Black Forest Cookies, page 78; Gingersnaps, page 62; Jam Jams, page 42; Chocolate Crinkles, page 64.

table of contents

the Company's Coming story

"never share a recipe you wouldn't use yourself"

Jean Paré (pronounced "jeen PAIR-ee") grew up understanding that the combination of family, friends and home cooking is the best recipe for a good life. From her mother, she learned to appreciate good cooking, while her father praised even her earliest attempts in the kitchen. When Jean left home, she took with her a love of cooking, many family recipes and an intriguing desire to read cookbooks as if they were novels!

When her four children had all reached school age, Jean volunteered to cater the 50th anniversary celebration of the Vermilion School of Agriculture, now Lakeland College, in Alberta, Canada. Working out of her home, Jean prepared a dinner for more than 1,000 people, launching a flourishing catering operation that continued for over 18 years. During that time, she had countless opportunities to test new ideas with immediate feedback—resulting in empty plates and contented customers! Whether preparing cocktail sandwiches for a house party or serving a hot meal for 1,500 people, Jean Paré earned a reputation for great food, courteous service and reasonable prices.

As requests for her recipes increased, Jean was often asked the question, "Why don't you write a cookbook?" Jean responded by teaming up with her son, Grant Lovig, in the fall of 1980 to form Company's Coming Publishing Limited. The publication of 150 Delicious Squares on April 14, 1981 marked the debut of what would soon become one of the world's most popular cookbook series.

The company has grown since those early days when Jean worked from a spare bedroom in her home. Today, she continues to write recipes while working closely with the staff of the Recipe Factory, as the Company's Coming test kitchen is affectionately known. There she fills the role of mentor, assisting with the development of recipes people most want to use for everyday cooking and easy entertaining. Every Company's Coming recipe is kitchen-tested before it is approved for publication.

Jean's daughter, Gail Lovig, is responsible for marketing and distribution, leading a team that includes sales personnel located in major cities across Canada. Company's Coming cookbooks are distributed in Canada, the United States, Australia and other world markets. Bestsellers many times over in English, Company's Coming cookbooks have also been published in French and Spanish.

Familiar and trusted in home kitchens around the world, Company's Coming cookbooks are offered in a variety of formats. Highly regarded as kitchen workbooks, the softcover Original Series, with its lay-flat plastic comb binding, is still a favourite among readers.

Jean Paré's approach to cooking has always called for quick and easy recipes using everyday ingredients. That view has served her well. The recipient of many awards, including the Queen Elizabeth Golden Jubilee Medal, Jean was appointed Member of the Order of Canada, her country's highest lifetime achievement honour.

Jean continues to gain new supporters by adhering to what she calls The Golden Rule of Cooking: Never share a recipe you wouldn't use yourself. It's an approach that has worked—millions of times over!

foreword

Cookies have been a part of the human experience for centuries. When Columbus sailed the ocean blue, he likely ate a cookie or two! Hardtack, made of unleavened flour and water, was dried to make a brittle, cracker-like "ship's biscuit." These biscuits stayed fresh for months and provided sustenance for sailors on long voyages. Over time, and quite by accident, the sweet biscuit we know today as the "cookie" evolved. Early bakers used small amounts of cake batter to test their oven's temperature. These small test cakes became known as "cookies." The rest, as they say, is history—cookies have been a favourite treat around the world ever since.

The first North American cookies were simple shortbread and butter cookies. As trade developed, ingredients such as coconut, nuts and chocolate were added. Modern conveniences and food processing methods led to the popularity of icebox cookies and cookies made with breakfast cereals. Ruth Wakefield of Massachusetts is credited with inventing the chocolate chip cookie at her Toll House Inn. She cut up a bar of semi-sweet chocolate and stirred the bits into her cookie dough, assuming they would melt during baking. Instead, the bits remained intact and the chocolate chip cookie was born—now one of North America's most-loved cookies!

Cookies are known around the world as biscuits, keks, teacakes and biscotti, and everyone has a favourite. We've baked dozens of cookies over the years and discovered many of our own favourites. We're pleased to present them to you in Most Loved Cookies. From everyday sweets to special occasion treats, you'll find a delightful assortment of drop, refrigerator, cut-out, shaped, pressed and no-bake treats in Most Loved Cookies, along with a variety of helpful tips and information. Let your family choose their favourites and make cookie history in your own kitchen.

Enjoy!

Jean Paré

nutrition information

Each recipe is analyzed using the most current version of the Canadian Nutrient File from Health Canada, which is based on the United States Department of Agriculture (USDA) Nutrient Database.

- If more than one ingredient is listed (such as "hard margarine or butter"), or if a range is given (1 – 2 tsp., 5 – 10 mL), only the first ingredient or first amount is analyzed.

- For meat, poultry and fish, the serving size per person is based on the recommended 4 oz. (113 g) uncooked weight (without bone), which is 2 – 3 oz. (57 – 85 g) cooked weight (without bone)— approximately the size of a deck of playing cards.

- Milk used is 1% M.F. (milk fat), unless otherwise stated.

- Cooking oil used is canola oil, unless otherwise stated.

- Ingredients indicating "sprinkle," "optional," or "for garnish" are not included in the nutrition information.

Margaret Ng, B.Sc. (Hon), M.A.
Registered Dietitian

No added spices—just plain good! These cookies are filled with fibre and flavour. Keep your cookie jar well-stocked with these tasty treats. Your family will be coming back for more.

Best Drop Cookies

Hard margarine (or butter), softened	1 cup	250 mL
Brown sugar, packed	1 1/2 cups	375 mL
Large eggs	2	2
Vanilla	1 tsp.	5 mL
All-purpose flour	2 cups	500 mL
Baking soda	1 tsp.	5 mL
Chopped pitted dates	1 lb.	454 g
Quick-cooking rolled oats (not instant)	1 cup	250 mL
Medium unsweetened coconut	1/2 cup	125 mL
Chopped walnuts	1/2 cup	125 mL
Quartered glazed cherries (optional)	1/2 cup	125 mL

Cream margarine and brown sugar in large bowl. Add eggs 1 at a time, beating well after each addition. Add vanilla. Beat until smooth.

Combine flour and baking soda in small bowl. Add to margarine mixture in 2 additions, mixing well after each addition until no dry flour remains.

Add remaining 5 ingredients. Mix well. Drop, using 1 1/2 tbsp. (25 mL) for each, about 2 inches (5 cm) apart onto greased cookie sheets. Bake in 350°F (175°C) oven for 10 to 12 minutes until golden. Remove to wire racks to cool. Makes about 5 dozen (60) cookies.

1 cookie: 109 Calories; 4.7 g Total Fat (2.4 g Mono, 0.8 g Poly, 1.2 g Sat); 7 mg Cholesterol; 16 g Carbohydrate; 1 g Fibre; 1 g Protein; 64 mg Sodium

Pictured on page 7.

An old favourite. These cookies get their name because they taste even better if they're hidden for a day or two after baking. Good luck—their spicy aroma is sure to bring any hermit out of hiding!

variation

Omit the raisins. Use the same amount of dried cranberries or chopped dried apricots.

Hermits

Hard margarine (or butter), softened	1 cup	250 mL
Brown sugar, packed	1 1/2 cups	375 mL
Large eggs	3	3
Vanilla	1 tsp.	5 mL
All-purpose flour	3 cups	750 mL
Baking powder	1 tsp.	5 mL
Baking soda	1 tsp.	5 mL
Ground cinnamon	1 tsp.	5 mL
Salt	1/2 tsp.	2 mL
Ground nutmeg	1/2 tsp.	2 mL
Ground allspice	1/4 tsp.	1 mL
Raisins	1 cup	250 mL
Chopped pitted dates	1 cup	250 mL
Chopped walnuts (or your favourite nuts)	2/3 cup	150 mL

Cream margarine and brown sugar in large bowl. Add eggs 1 at a time, beating well after each addition. Add vanilla. Beat until smooth.

Combine next 7 ingredients in medium bowl. Add to margarine mixture in 3 additions, mixing well after each addition until no dry flour remains.

Add remaining 3 ingredients. Mix well. Drop, using 1 1/2 tbsp. (25 mL) for each, about 2 inches (5 cm) apart onto greased cookie sheets. Bake in 375°F (190°C) oven for 6 to 8 minutes until golden. Let stand for 5 minutes. Remove to wire racks to cool. Makes about 4 dozen (48) cookies.

1 cookie: 130 Calories; 5.5 g Total Fat (3 g Mono, 1.2 g Poly, 1 g Sat); 13 mg Cholesterol; 19 g Carbohydrate; 1 g Fibre; 2 g Protein; 114 mg Sodium

Pictured on page 9.

about cloves

Cloves are the dried flower buds of the tropical clove evergreen tree. In cookies and baked goods, ground cloves have a pungent aroma reminiscent of Christmas, but are good any time of the year.

Pumpkin Cookies

Hard margarine (or butter), softened	1/2 cup	125 mL
Brown sugar, packed	1 1/4 cups	300 mL
Large eggs	2	2
Canned pure pumpkin (no spices)	1 cup	250 mL
Vanilla	1 tsp.	5 mL
All-purpose flour	2 cups	500 mL
Baking powder	4 tsp.	20 mL
Salt	1/2 tsp.	2 mL
Ground cinnamon	1/2 tsp.	2 mL
Ground nutmeg	1/2 tsp.	2 mL
Ground cloves	1/4 tsp.	1 mL
Ground ginger	1/4 tsp.	1 mL
Raisins (or semi-sweet chocolate chips)	1 cup	250 mL
Chopped walnuts (or your favourite nuts)	1 cup	250 mL

Cream margarine and brown sugar in large bowl. Add eggs 1 at a time, beating well after each addition. Add pumpkin and vanilla. Beat until smooth.

Combine next 7 ingredients in small bowl. Add to margarine mixture in 2 additions, mixing well after each addition until no dry flour remains.

Add raisins and walnuts. Mix well. Drop, using 1 1/2 tbsp. (25 mL) for each, about 2 inches (5 cm) apart onto greased cookie sheets. Bake in 375°F (190°C) oven for about 15 minutes until golden. Let stand on cookie sheets for 5 minutes before removing to wire racks to cool. Makes about 4 dozen (48) cookies.

1 cookie: 93 Calories; 3.9 g Total Fat (1.8 g Mono, 1.3 g Poly, 0.6 g Sat); 9 mg Cholesterol; 14 g Carbohydrate; 1 g Fibre; 2 g Protein; 85 mg Sodium

Pictured on page 13.

Spicy Dads

Hard margarine (or butter), softened	1 cup	250 mL
Granulated sugar	1 cup	250 mL
Brown sugar, packed	1/2 cup	125 mL
Large egg	1	1
Fancy (mild) molasses	2 tbsp.	30 mL
Vanilla	1 tsp.	5 mL
All-purpose flour	1 1/2 cups	375 mL
Baking powder	1 tsp.	5 mL
Baking soda	1 tsp.	5 mL
Ground cinnamon	1 tsp.	5 mL
Ground nutmeg	1 tsp.	5 mL
Ground allspice	1 tsp.	5 mL
Quick-cooking rolled oats (not instant)	1 1/2 cups	375 mL
Medium unsweetened coconut	1 cup	250 mL

Cream margarine and both sugars in large bowl. Add egg. Beat well. Add molasses and vanilla. Beat until smooth.

Combine next 6 ingredients in small bowl. Add to margarine mixture in 2 additions, mixing well after each addition until no dry flour remains.

Add rolled oats and coconut. Mix well. Drop, using 1 tbsp. (15 mL) for each, about 2 inches (5 cm) apart onto greased cookie sheets. Flatten slightly. Bake in 300°F (150°C) oven for about 12 minutes until golden. Let stand on cookie sheets for 5 minutes before removing to wire racks to cool. Makes about 5 dozen (60) cookies.

1 cookie: 86 Calories; 4.6 g Total Fat (2.2 g Mono, 0.4 g Poly, 1.6 g Sat); 4 mg Cholesterol; 11 g Carbohydrate; trace Fibre; 1 g Protein; 68 mg Sodium

Pictured on page 13.

A spicier version of the commercial kind. Always good. Not only for Dad—the kids will love them, too!

about allspice

Did you know that allspice is a berry from a tree? It's called allspice because it tastes like a blend of cinnamon, nutmeg and cloves.

The enticing aroma of these carrot cookies wafting through the house will lead everyone by the nose to see what's up!

carrot ginger cookies

Crystallized ginger adds a sweet, spicy flavour to cookies. Use sparingly—it has quite a bite! In this recipe, add 1/4 cup (60 mL) minced crystallized ginger with the rolled oats and raisins.

Carrot Cookies

Hard margarine (or butter), softened	1/2 cup	125 mL
Granulated sugar	1 cup	250 mL
Large egg	1	1
Cooked mashed carrot	1 cup	250 mL
Milk	1/3 cup	75 mL
Vanilla	1 tsp.	5 mL
All-purpose flour	2 cups	500 mL
Baking powder	2 tsp.	10 mL
Ground cinnamon	1 tsp.	5 mL
Salt	1/4 tsp.	1 mL
Quick-cooking rolled oats (not instant)	2 cups	500 mL
Raisins	1 cup	250 mL
ORANGE ICING		
Icing (confectioner's) sugar	2 1/2 cups	625 mL
Hard margarine (or butter), softened	1/3 cup	75 mL
Orange juice	2 tbsp.	30 mL
Grated orange zest	1 1/2 tbsp.	25 mL

Cream margarine and sugar in large bowl. Add egg. Beat well. Add carrot, milk and vanilla. Beat until smooth.

Combine next 4 ingredients in small bowl. Add to margarine mixture in 2 additions, mixing well after each addition until no dry flour remains.

Add rolled oats and raisins. Mix well. Drop, using 1 tbsp. (15 mL) for each, about 2 inches (5 cm) apart onto greased cookie sheets. Bake in 375°F (190°C) oven for 12 to 15 minutes until golden. Remove to wire racks to cool completely.

Orange Icing: Beat all 4 ingredients in medium bowl, adding more icing sugar or orange juice if necessary until spreading consistency. Makes about 1 1/2 cups (375 mL) icing. Spread about 1 tbsp. (15 mL) icing on top of each cookie. Makes about 5 dozen (60) cookies.

1 cookie: 100 Calories; 3.1 g Total Fat (1.9 g Mono, 0.4 g Poly, 0.6 g Sat); 4 mg Cholesterol; 7 g Carbohydrate; 1 g Fibre; 1 g Protein; 59 mg Sodium

Pictured on page 13.

Top left: Pumpkin Cookies, page 10
Top right: Spicy Dads, page 11
Bottom: Carrot Cookies, above

For chocolate fans! Walnuts give these soft cookies a bit of pizzazz, but they're just as good without them.

Chocolate Softies

Hard margarine (or butter), softened	1/2 cup	125 mL
Granulated sugar	1 cup	250 mL
Large egg	1	1
Unsweetened chocolate baking squares (1 oz., 28 g, each), chopped	2	2
Sour milk (see Note)	1/3 cup	75 mL
Vanilla	1 tsp.	5 mL
All-purpose flour	1 3/4 cups	425 mL
Baking soda	1/2 tsp.	2 mL
Salt	1/2 tsp.	2 mL
Chopped walnuts (optional)	1/2 cup	125 mL
CHOCOLATE ICING		
Icing (confectioner's) sugar	1 1/4 cups	300 mL
Cocoa, sifted if lumpy	1/3 cup	75 mL
Hard margarine (or butter), softened	3 tbsp.	50 mL
Hot strong prepared coffee (or water)	1 1/2 tbsp.	25 mL

Cream margarine and sugar in large bowl. Add egg. Beat well.

Heat chocolate in small heavy saucepan on lowest heat, stirring often until almost melted. Do not overheat. Remove from heat. Stir until smooth. Add to margarine mixture. Add sour milk and vanilla. Stir well.

Combine flour, baking soda and salt in small bowl. Add to chocolate mixture in 2 additions, mixing well after each addition until no dry flour remains.

Add walnuts. Mix well. Drop, using 1 tbsp. (15 mL) for each, about 2 inches (5 cm) apart onto ungreased cookie sheets. Bake in 350°F (175°C) oven for 10 to 12 minutes until firm. Let stand on cookie sheets for 5 minutes before removing to wire racks to cool completely.

Chocolate Icing: Beat all 4 ingredients in medium bowl, adding more icing sugar or coffee if necessary until spreading consistency. Makes about 2 cups (500 mL) icing. Spread about 2 tsp. (10 mL) icing on top of each cookie. Makes about 4 dozen (48) cookies.

1 cookie: 82 Calories; 3.6 g Total Fat (2.1 g Mono, 0.3 g Poly, 1.1 g Sat); 5 mg Cholesterol; 12 g Carbohydrate; 1 g Fibre; 1 g Protein; 73 mg Sodium

Pictured on page 15.

Dipper some Chippers in a glass of cold milk!

decadent chocolate chippers

Turn Chocolate Chippers into decadent dunkers! Omit the chocolate chips, use 3 cups (750 mL) chocolate chunks, and increase the walnuts to 2 cups (500 mL).

Pictured on front cover.

chipper pizza

Make cookie dough according to the recipe. Press dough evenly in greased 12 inch (30 cm) pizza pan. Sprinkle with:

1/2 cup (125 mL) candy-coated chocolate candies (such as Smarties or M & M's)

1/3 cup (75 mL) butterscotch chips

1/4 cup (60 mL) cornflakes cereal

1/4 cup (60 mL) peanuts

2 tbsp. (30 mL) medium sweetened coconut

1 tbsp. (15 mL) toffee bits (such as Skor or Heath Bar)

Bake in 350°F (175°C) oven for 12 to 15 minutes until golden.

Pictured on page 17.

Chocolate Chippers

Hard margarine (or butter), softened	1 cup	250 mL
Brown sugar, packed	1 1/2 cups	375 mL
Large eggs	2	2
Vanilla	1 tsp.	5 mL
All-purpose flour	2 cups	500 mL
Cornstarch	1/4 cup	60 mL
Baking soda	1 tsp.	5 mL
Salt	3/4 tsp.	4 mL
Semi-sweet chocolate chips	2 cups	500 mL
Coarsely chopped walnuts (optional)	1 cup	250 mL

Cream margarine and brown sugar in large bowl. Add eggs 1 at a time, beating well after each addition. Add vanilla. Beat until smooth.

Combine next 4 ingredients in small bowl. Add to margarine mixture in 2 additions, mixing well after each addition until no dry flour remains.

Add chocolate chips and walnuts. Mix well. Drop, using 1 1/2 tbsp. (25 mL) for each, about 2 inches (5 cm) apart onto greased cookie sheets. Bake in 350°F (175°C) oven for 10 to 15 minutes until golden. Let stand on cookie sheets for 5 minutes before removing to wire racks to cool. Makes about 3 dozen (36) cookies.

1 cookie: 166 Calories; 8.7 g Total Fat (4.6 g Mono, 0.7 g Poly, 3 g Sat); 12 mg Cholesterol; 22 g Carbohydrate; 1 g Fibre; 2 g Protein; 157 mg Sodium

Pictured on page 17.

Top: Chipper Pizza, this page
Bottom: Chocolate Chippers, above

For cherry lovers—a soft, golden cookie filled with cherries, dates, nuts and coconut.

Cherry Snacks

Hard margarine (or butter), softened	1 cup	250 mL
Granulated sugar	3/4 cup	175 mL
All-purpose flour	2 cups	500 mL
Salt	1/2 tsp.	2 mL
Boiling water	1/4 cup	60 mL
Baking soda	1 tsp.	5 mL
Chopped pitted dates	1 cup	250 mL
Chopped walnuts	1 cup	250 mL
Chopped glazed cherries	1 cup	250 mL
Medium unsweetened coconut	3/4 cup	175 mL

Cream margarine and sugar in large bowl. Add flour and salt. Mix until no dry flour remains.

Stir boiling water into baking soda in small bowl until dissolved. Add to margarine mixture. Stir well.

Add remaining 4 ingredients. Mix well. Drop, using 1 tbsp. (15 mL) for each, about 2 inches (5 cm) apart onto greased cookie sheets. Bake in 350°F (175°C) oven for 12 to 15 minutes until golden. Remove to wire racks to cool. Makes about 4 dozen (48) cookies.

1 cookie: 119 Calories; 6.6 g Total Fat (3 g Mono, 1.5 g Poly, 1.8 g Sat); 0 mg Cholesterol; 15 g Carbohydrate; 1 g Fibre; 1 g Protein; 100 mg Sodium

Pictured on pages 20/21 and on back cover.

Make a double batch and keep some in the freezer. They're always good for rounding out a lunch box, and equally appreciated at snack time after school.

Oatmeal Raisin Cookies

Hard margarine (or butter), softened	1 cup	250 mL
Brown sugar, packed	1 cup	250 mL
Large egg	1	1
Vanilla	1 tsp.	5 mL
All-purpose flour	1 1/2 cups	375 mL
Baking soda	1 tsp.	5 mL
Salt	1/4 tsp.	1 mL
Quick-cooking rolled oats (not instant)	1 1/4 cups	300 mL
Raisins	1 cup	250 mL

(continued on next page)

Cream margarine and brown sugar in large bowl. Add egg. Beat well. Add vanilla. Beat until smooth.

Combine flour, baking soda and salt in small bowl. Add to margarine mixture in 2 additions, mixing well after each addition until no dry flour remains.

Add rolled oats and raisins. Mix well. Drop, using 1 tbsp. (15 mL) for each, about 2 inches (5 cm) apart onto greased cookie sheets. Bake in 350°F (175°C) oven for 8 to 10 minutes until golden. Let stand on cookie sheets for 5 minutes before removing to wire racks to cool. Makes about 3 1/2 dozen (42) cookies.

1 cookie: 104 Calories; 5 g Total Fat (3.1 g Mono, 0.6 g Poly, 1 g Sat); 5 mg Cholesterol; 14 g Carbohydrate; 1 g Fibre; 1 g Protein; 103 mg Sodium

Pictured on page 201 and on back cover.

> **tip**
>
> To prevent cookies from sticking together during freezing, layer completely cooled cookies between sheets of waxed paper in an airtight container. Freeze for up to 3 months.

Chocolate Nuggets

Tasty chocolate morsels with a brownie-like texture. Yum!

Semi-sweet chocolate chips	2 cups	500 mL
Can of sweetened condensed milk	11 oz.	300 mL
Hard margarine (or butter)	1/4 cup	60 mL
Granulated sugar	1/4 cup	60 mL
Vanilla	1 tsp.	5 mL
All-purpose flour	1 cup	250 mL
Chopped walnuts (or your favourite nuts), optional	1/2 cup	125 mL

Heat first 5 ingredients in heavy medium saucepan on lowest heat, stirring often until chocolate chips are almost melted. Do not overheat. Remove from heat. Stir until smooth.

Add flour and walnuts. Mix until no dry flour remains. Drop, using 1 tsp. (5 mL) for each, about 2 inches (5 cm) apart onto greased cookie sheets. Bake in 350°F (175°C) oven for 10 to 12 minutes until dry. Cookies will be soft. Let stand on cookie sheets for 5 minutes before removing to wire racks to cool. Makes about 6 dozen (72) cookies.

1 cookie: 57 Calories; 2.6 g Total Fat (1.1 g Mono, 0.1 g Poly, 1.3 g Sat); 2 mg Cholesterol; 8 g Carbohydrate; trace Fibre; 1 g Protein; 15 mg Sodium

Pictured on page 21 and on back cover.

Photo legend, next page
Top left: Oatmeal Raisin Cookies, page 18
Top right: Cherry Snacks, page 18
Bottom right: Chocolate Nuggets, this page
Bottom left: Gumdrop Cookies, page 22

Goody, goody, gumdrops! Dotted with colourful candy, these won't last long.

tip

If your cookies are brown on the bottom but not cooked through, move the cookie sheet to a higher rack in the oven, or add insulation by slipping a second cookie sheet under the first.

Gumdrop Cookies

Hard margarine (or butter), softened	1 cup	250 mL
Brown sugar, packed	1 cup	250 mL
Granulated sugar	1/4 cup	60 mL
Large eggs	2	2
Vanilla	1 tsp.	5 mL
All-purpose flour	1 1/2 cups	375 mL
Baking powder	1 tsp.	5 mL
Baking soda	1/2 tsp.	2 mL
Salt	1/2 tsp.	2 mL
Quick-cooking rolled oats (not instant)	1 cup	250 mL
Chopped gumdrops (no black)	1 cup	250 mL
Chopped nuts (your favourite), optional	1/2 cup	125 mL

Cream margarine and both sugars in large bowl. Add eggs 1 at a time, beating well after each addition. Add vanilla. Beat until smooth.

Combine next 4 ingredients in small bowl. Add to margarine mixture in 2 additions, mixing well after each addition until no dry flour remains.

Add remaining 3 ingredients. Mix well. Drop, using 1 tbsp. (15 mL) for each, about 2 inches (5 cm) apart onto ungreased cookie sheets. Bake in 350°F (175°C) oven for 12 to 14 minutes until golden. Let stand on cookie sheets for 5 minutes before removing to wire racks to cool. Makes about 4 dozen (48) cookies.

1 cookie: 101 Calories; 4.4 g Total Fat (2.8 g Mono, 0.5 g Poly, 0.9 g Sat); 9 mg Cholesterol; 15 g Carbohydrate; trace Fibre; 1 g Protein; 99 mg Sodium

Pictured on page 201 and on back cover.

The perfect macaroon—sweet and chewy in the middle, crispy on the outside. Drizzle these with melted chocolate for an extra-special treat.

Macaroons

Granulated sugar	3/4 cup	175 mL
Cornstarch	2 tbsp.	30 mL
Salt	1/8 tsp.	0.5 mL
Egg whites (large)	3	3
Shredded (long thread) coconut	4 cups	1 L

(continued on next page)

Combine sugar, cornstarch and salt in small bowl.

Beat egg whites on high in top of double boiler or large heatproof bowl for about 5 minutes until stiff, dry peaks form. Place over boiling water in double boiler or medium saucepan. Add sugar mixture in 3 additions, beating on medium-high for about 1 minute until smooth and glossy. Cook for about 6 minutes, without stirring, until dry crust forms around edge.

Fold meringue into coconut in large bowl until well combined. Drop, using 2 tsp. (10 mL) for each, about 2 inches (5 cm) apart onto greased cookie sheets. Bake in 350°F (175°C) oven for about 12 minutes until golden. Let stand on cookie sheets for 5 minutes before removing to wire racks to cool. Makes about 4 dozen (48) macaroons.

1 macaroon: 67 Calories; 5.1 g Total Fat (0.2 g Mono, 0.1 g Poly, 4.5 g Sat); 0 mg Cholesterol; 6 g Carbohydrate; trace Fibre; 1 g Protein; 13 mg Sodium

Pictured below.

Top: Macaroons, page 22
Bottom: White Chip Cookies, page 24

A new chip off the old block. White chocolate chips peek through this dark chocolate cookie. Scrumptious.

variation

One recipe—endless possibilities! Instead of white chocolate chips, use other chips such as milk chocolate, mint chocolate, butterscotch or peanut butter.

White Chip Cookies

Hard margarine (or butter), softened	1/2 cup	125 mL
Brown sugar, packed	1 cup	250 mL
Cocoa, sifted if lumpy	1/2 cup	125 mL
Large egg	1	1
Vanilla	1 tsp.	5 mL
All-purpose flour	1 cup	250 mL
Baking soda	1/2 tsp.	2 mL
Salt	1/2 tsp.	2 mL
White chocolate chips	1 cup	250 mL
Chopped walnuts (or pecans), optional	3/4 cup	175 mL

Cream margarine and brown sugar in large bowl. Add cocoa. Beat well. Add egg and vanilla. Beat until smooth.

Combine flour, baking soda and salt in small bowl. Add to margarine mixture. Mix until no dry flour remains.

Add white chocolate chips and walnuts. Mix well. Drop, using 1 tbsp. (15 mL) for each, about 2 inches (5 cm) apart onto greased cookie sheets. Flatten slightly. Bake in 350°F (175°C) oven for 10 to 12 minutes until firm. Let stand on cookie sheets for 5 minutes before removing to wire racks to cool. Makes about 3 dozen (36) cookies.

1 cookie: 94 Calories; 4.6 g Total Fat (2.3 g Mono, 0.4 g Poly, 1.6 g Sat); 7 mg Cholesterol; 13 g Carbohydrate; 1 g Fibre; 1 g Protein; 91 mg Sodium

Pictured on page 23.

The goodness of bran and nuts in a not-too-sweet treat. Good with or without cinnamon.

Bran Cereal Cookies

Hard margarine (or butter), softened	1 cup	250 mL
Granulated sugar	1 cup	250 mL
Large eggs	2	2
Vanilla	1 1/2 tsp.	7 mL

(continued on next page)

All-purpose flour	1 1/2 cups	375 mL
Baking soda	1 tsp.	5 mL
Ground cinnamon (optional)	1 tsp.	5 mL
Salt	1/2 tsp.	2 mL
All-bran cereal	1 1/2 cups	375 mL
Chopped walnuts (or your favourite nuts)	1 cup	250 mL

tip

To soften cookies, place them in an airtight container with a quarter of a fresh apple for 24 hours. The cookies will become moist and have a subtle apple flavour.

Cream margarine and sugar in large bowl. Add eggs 1 at a time, beating well after each addition. Add vanilla. Beat until smooth.

Combine next 4 ingredients in small bowl. Add to margarine mixture in 2 additions, mixing well after each addition until no dry flour remains.

Add cereal and walnuts. Mix well. Drop, using 1 tbsp. (15 mL) for each, about 2 inches (5 cm) apart onto greased cookie sheets. Bake in 375°F (190°C) oven for 12 to 14 minutes until golden. Remove to wire racks to cool. Makes about 4 1/2 dozen (54) cookies.

1 cookie: 83 Calories; 5.2 g Total Fat (2.7 g Mono, 1.3 g Poly, 0.9 g Sat); 8 mg Cholesterol; 9 g Carbohydrate; 1 g Fibre; 1 g Protein; 108 mg Sodium

Pictured below.

Cheery cherry cookies are so hard to resist!

note

To toast nuts, spread them evenly in an ungreased shallow pan. Bake in a 350ºF (175ºC) oven for 5 to 10 minutes, stirring or shaking often, until desired doneness.

cherry pecan butter cookies

Omit the slivered almonds. Use the same amount of pecan pieces.

Cherry Almond Butter Cookies

Butter (not margarine), softened	2 cups	500 mL
Granulated sugar	1 1/2 cups	375 mL
Large egg	1	1
Vanilla	2 tsp.	10 mL
All-purpose flour	5 cups	1.25 L
Baking powder	2 tsp.	10 mL
Salt	1/2 tsp.	2 mL
Dried cherries	1 1/3 cups	325 mL
Slivered almonds, toasted (see Note)	1 cup	250 mL

Cream butter and sugar in large bowl. Add egg. Beat well. Add vanilla. Beat until smooth.

Combine flour, baking powder and salt in medium bowl. Add to butter mixture in 3 additions, mixing well after each addition until no dry flour remains.

Add cherries. Mix well. Divide dough into 3 equal portions. Shape each portion into 8 inch (20 cm) long log. Wrap each log with waxed paper. Chill for at least 6 hours or overnight. Discard waxed paper from 1 log. Cut into 1/3 inch (1 cm) slices. Arrange about 2 inches (5 cm) apart on greased cookie sheets.

Gently press 2 or 3 almond slivers in decorative pattern on top of each slice. Bake in 350ºF (175ºC) oven for about 10 minutes until just golden. Let stand on cookie sheets for 5 minutes before removing to wire racks to cool. Repeat with remaining logs and almond slivers. Makes about 6 dozen (72) cookies.

1 cookie: 119 Calories; 6.7 g Total Fat (2.3 g Mono, 0.5 g Poly, 3.5 g Sat); 18 mg Cholesterol; 14 g Carbohydrate; 1 g Fibre; 2 g Protein; 83 mg Sodium

Pictured on page 27.

Buttery shortbread gets a chocolate spin. Prepare the dough one day and bake it the next.

checkerboard shortbread

Divide chocolate dough into 2 equal portions. Repeat with white dough. Shape each portion into 12 inch (30 cm) long rope. Position all 4 ropes as shown in Diagram B. Wrap together with waxed paper. Chill, cut and bake as directed.

Pictured on page 29 and on back cover.

cloverleaf shortbread

Omit cocoa. Divide entire amount of dough into 3 equal portions. Colour 1 portion yellow, 1 pink and 1 green with drops of liquid food colouring. Shape each portion into 12 inch (30 cm) long rope. Position all 3 ropes as shown in Diagram C. Wrap together with waxed paper. Chill, cut and bake as directed.

Pictured on page 29 and on back cover.

Shortbread Pinwheels

Butter (not margarine), softened	1 cup	250 mL
Icing (confectioner's) sugar	2/3 cup	150 mL
Vanilla	1/2 tsp.	2 mL
All-purpose flour	2 cups	500 mL
Cocoa, sifted if lumpy	1/4 cup	60 mL

Beat butter, icing sugar and vanilla in medium bowl until smooth. Add flour in 2 additions, mixing well after each addition until no dry flour remains. Divide dough into 2 equal portions.

Add cocoa to 1 dough portion. Mix until evenly coloured. Roll out chocolate dough between 2 sheets of waxed paper to 7 x 12 inch (18 x 30 cm) rectangle. Repeat with remaining dough portion. Discard top sheet of waxed paper from both rectangles. Flip 1 rectangle onto the other, aligning edges of dough as evenly as possible. Discard top sheet of waxed paper. Roll up tightly from long side, jelly roll-style, using waxed paper as a guide (see Diagram A). Wrap with same sheet of waxed paper. Chill for at least 6 hours or overnight. Discard waxed paper. Cut into 1/3 inch (1 cm) slices. Arrange about 2 inches (5 cm) apart on ungreased cookie sheets. Bake in 350ºF (175ºC) oven for 10 to 12 minutes until firm. Let stand on cookie sheets for 5 minutes before removing to wire racks to cool. Makes about 3 dozen (36) cookies.

1 cookie: 85 Calories; 5.6 g Total Fat (1.6 g Mono, 0.2 g Poly, 3.4 g Sat); 15 mg Cholesterol; 8 g Carbohydrate; trace Fibre; 1 g Protein; 55 mg Sodium

Pictured on page 29 and on back cover.

Diagram A
(Pinwheel)

Diagram B
(Checkerboard)

Diagram C
(Cloverleaf)

Top: Shortbread Pinwheels, above
Bottom right: Checkerboard Shortbread, this page
Bottom left: Cloverleaf Shortbread, this page

Simply delicious. Makes a huge batch for stocking up the freezer.

an added touch

Drizzle melted butterscotch chips in a decorative pattern over the baked cookies.

Butterscotch Cookies

Hard margarine (or butter), softened	1 cup	250 mL
Brown sugar, packed	2 cups	500 mL
Large eggs	2	2
Vanilla	1 tsp.	5 mL
All-purpose flour	3 cups	750 mL
Baking soda	1 tsp.	5 mL
Chopped walnuts	1 cup	250 mL

Cream margarine and brown sugar in large bowl. Add eggs 1 at a time, beating well after each addition. Add vanilla. Beat until smooth.

Combine flour and baking soda in medium bowl. Add to margarine mixture in 3 additions, mixing well after each addition until no dry flour remains.

Add walnuts. Mix well. Divide dough into 4 equal portions. Shape each portion into 9 inch (22 cm) long log. Wrap each log with waxed paper. Chill for at least 6 hours or overnight. Discard waxed paper from 1 log. Cut into 1/4 inch (6 mm) slices. Arrange about 2 inches (5 cm) apart on ungreased cookie sheets. Bake in 350°F (175°C) oven for 8 to 10 minutes until golden. Let stand on cookie sheets for 5 minutes before removing to wire racks to cool. Repeat with remaining logs. Makes about 12 dozen (144) cookies.

1 cookie: 41 Calories; 2 g Total Fat (1 g Mono, 0.5 g Poly, 0.3 g Sat); 3 mg Cholesterol; 5 g Carbohydrate; trace Fibre; 1 g Protein; 27 mg Sodium

Pictured on page 31.

These pastry-like cookies topped with your favourite jam or marmalade are sure to please.

Cream Cheese Cookies

Hard margarine (or butter), softened	1/2 cup	125 mL
Granulated sugar	1/3 cup	75 mL
Cream cheese, softened	1/4 cup	60mL
Vanilla	1/2 tsp.	2 mL
All-purpose flour	1 cup	250 mL
Jam (or marmalade), your favourite, approximately	1 cup	250 mL

(continued on next page)

Cream margarine and sugar in medium bowl. Add cream cheese. Beat well. Add vanilla. Beat until smooth.

Add flour. Mix until no dry flour remains. Divide dough into 2 equal portions. Shape each portion into 5 inch (12.5 cm) long log. Wrap each log with waxed paper. Chill for at least 6 hours or overnight. Discard waxed paper from 1 log. Cut into 1/4 inch (6 mm) slices. Arrange about 2 inches (5 cm) apart on ungreased cookie sheets.

Spoon about 1 tsp. (5 mL) jam onto centre of each slice. Bake in 350°F (175°C) oven for 8 to 10 minutes until golden. Let stand on cookie sheets for 5 minutes before removing to wire racks to cool. Repeat with remaining log and jam. Makes about 3 dozen (36) cookies.

1 cookie: 74 Calories; 3.3 g Total Fat (1.9 g Mono, 0.3 g Poly, 0.9 g Sat); 2 mg Cholesterol; 11 g Carbohydrate; trace Fibre; 1 g Protein; 40 mg Sodium

Pictured below.

cream cheese crescents

Prepare dough as directed. Flatten logs slightly before wrapping and chilling. Roll out 1 portion on lightly floured surface to 8 x 10 inch (20 x 25 cm) rectangle. Cut into 2 inch (5 cm) squares. Spread jam onto each square, leaving 1/4 inch (6 mm) edge. Roll up diagonally from 1 corner toward opposite corner to enclose jam. Bend both ends slightly to form crescent shape. Bake as directed. Repeat with remaining dough and jam. Makes about 40 crescents.

Left: Butterscotch Cookies, page 30
Right: Cream Cheese Cookies, page 30

For peanut butter and jam fans. These crisp, golden cookies are perfect with a glass of cold milk.

PBJ Crisps

Hard margarine (or butter), softened	1/2 cup	125 mL
Granulated sugar	1/2 cup	125 mL
Smooth peanut butter	1/2 cup	125 mL
Raspberry jam	1/2 cup	125 mL
Large egg	1	1
Vanilla	1 tsp.	5 mL
All-purpose flour	2 1/2 cups	625 mL
Baking powder	1 1/2 tsp.	7 mL
Baking soda	1/2 tsp.	2 mL
Salt	1/2 tsp.	2 mL
Coarsely chopped peanuts	1/2 cup	125 mL

Cream margarine and sugar in large bowl. Add peanut butter and jam. Beat until well combined.

Add egg and vanilla. Beat until smooth.

Combine next 4 ingredients in medium bowl. Add to margarine mixture in 2 additions, mixing well after each addition until no dry flour remains.

Add peanuts. Mix well. Divide dough into 2 equal portions. Shape each portion into 8 inch (20 cm) long log. Wrap each log with waxed paper. Chill for at least 6 hours or overnight. Discard waxed paper from 1 log. Cut into 1/4 inch (6 mm) slices. Arrange about 2 inches (5 cm) apart on greased cookie sheets. Bake in 350°F (175°C) oven for about 12 minutes until golden. Let stand on cookie sheets for 5 minutes before removing to wire racks to cool. Repeat with remaining log. Makes about 5 dozen (60) cookies.

1 cookie: 69 Calories; 3.4 g Total Fat (1.9 g Mono, 0.7 g Poly, 0.7 g Sat); 4 mg Cholesterol; 8 g Carbohydrate; trace Fibre; 2 g Protein; 72 mg Sodium

Pictured on page 33.

An old favourite—lots of variations.

raspberry pinwheels

Prepare and roll out cookie dough as directed. Omit the date mixture. On each dough portion, spread 2 tbsp. (30 mL) raspberry jam, leaving 1/2 inch (12 mm) edge. Sprinkle 2 tbsp. (30 mL) shredded (long thread) coconut and 1 tbsp. (15 mL) finely chopped walnuts (or your favourite nuts) over jam. Roll up, jelly roll-style, and wrap with waxed paper. Chill, slice and bake as directed.

Pictured on page 35.

chocolate pinwheels

Prepare and roll out cookie dough as directed. Omit the date mixture. Heat 1/2 cup (125 mL) semi-sweet chocolate chips in a small heavy saucepan on lowest heat, stirring often until almost melted. Do not overheat. Remove from heat. Stir until smooth. On each dough portion, spread about 2 tbsp. (30 mL) chocolate, leaving 1/2 inch (12 mm) edge. Roll up, jelly roll-style, and wrap with waxed paper. Chill until chocolate is set. Bring rolls to room temperature before slicing and baking as directed.

Pictured on page 35.

Date Pinwheels

Chopped pitted dates	1 lb.	454 g
Granulated sugar	1/2 cup	125 mL
Water	1/3 cup	75 mL
Finely chopped walnuts	2/3 cup	150 mL
Hard margarine (or butter), softened	1 cup	250 mL
Brown sugar, packed	1 cup	250 mL
Granulated sugar	1 cup	250 mL
Large eggs	2	2
Vanilla	2 tsp.	10 mL
All-purpose flour	3 1/2 cups	875 mL
Baking soda	1 tsp.	5 mL
Salt	1/2 tsp.	2 mL

Combine dates, first amount of granulated sugar and water in medium saucepan. Bring to a boil on medium. Reduce heat to medium-low. Simmer, uncovered, for about 10 minutes, stirring occasionally, adding more water if necessary while simmering, until dates are softened. Remove from heat. Add walnuts. Stir. Let stand for 10 minutes.

Cream margarine, brown sugar and second amount of granulated sugar in large bowl. Add eggs 1 at a time, beating well after each addition. Add vanilla. Beat until smooth.

Combine flour, baking soda and salt in medium bowl. Add to margarine mixture in 3 additions, mixing well after each addition until no dry flour remains. Divide dough into 4 equal portions. Roll out 1 portion between 2 sheets of waxed paper to 8 inch (20 cm) square. Discard top sheet of waxed paper. Spread about 1/4 of date mixture evenly on dough, leaving 1/2 inch (12 mm) edge. Roll up tightly, jelly roll-style, using waxed paper as a guide. Wrap with same sheet of waxed paper. Repeat with remaining dough portions and date mixture, wrapping each roll with waxed paper. Chill for at least 6 hours or overnight. Discard waxed paper from 1 roll. Cut into 1/4 inch (6 mm) slices. Arrange about 2 inches (5 cm) apart on greased cookie sheets. Bake in 375°F (190°C) oven for 8 to 10 minutes until golden. Let stand on cookie sheets for 5 minutes before removing to wire racks to cool. Repeat with remaining rolls. Makes about 10 1/2 dozen (126) pinwheels.

1 pinwheel: 59 Calories; 2.1 g Total Fat (1.1 g Mono, 0.4 g Poly, 0.4 g Sat); 3 mg Cholesterol; 10 g Carbohydrate; trace Fibre; 1 g Protein; 40 mg Sodium

Pictured on page 35.

Top: Raspberry Pinwheels, this page
Centre: Date Pinwheels, above
Bottom: Chocolate Pinwheels, this page

Deliciously crisp, with a lovely citrus glaze drizzled on top. A nice tea time cookie.

chocolate-dipped lemon cookies

Prepare and shape dough as directed. Slightly flatten both round logs to create squared logs. Chill, cut and bake as directed. Omit Lemon Glaze.

Heat 3 chopped 1 oz. (28 g) squares of semi-sweet chocolate in a small heavy saucepan on lowest heat, stirring often until chocolate is almost melted. Do not overheat. Remove from heat. Stir until smooth. Transfer to a small custard cup. Dip cookies halfway into chocolate. Place on a waxed paper-lined cookie sheet. Let stand until set.

Pictured on page 37.

Lemon Icebox Cookies

Hard margarine (or butter), softened	1 cup	250 mL
Granulated sugar	3/4 cup	175 mL
Large eggs	2	2
Grated lemon zest	1 tbsp.	15 mL
All-purpose flour	3 cups	750 mL
Baking powder	1/2 tsp.	2 mL
Salt	1/4 tsp.	1 mL
LEMON GLAZE		
Lemon juice	1 – 2 tbsp.	15 – 30 mL
Icing (confectioner's) sugar	1/2 cup	125 mL
Drop of yellow liquid food colouring (optional)	1	1

Cream margarine and sugar in large bowl. Add eggs 1 at a time, beating well after each addition. Add lemon zest. Beat until smooth.

Combine flour, baking powder and salt in medium bowl. Add to margarine mixture in 3 additions, mixing well after each addition until no dry flour remains. Divide dough into 2 equal portions. Shape each portion into 8 inch (20 cm) long log. Wrap each log with waxed paper. Chill for at least 6 hours or overnight. Discard waxed paper from 1 log. Cut into 1/4 inch (6 mm) slices. Arrange about 2 inches (5 cm) apart on ungreased cookie sheets. Bake in 375°F (190°C) oven for 7 to 10 minutes until golden. Let stand on cookie sheets for 5 minutes before removing to wire racks to cool completely. Repeat with remaining log.

Lemon Glaze: Stir lemon juice into icing sugar in small bowl, adding more lemon juice or icing sugar if necessary until pourable consistency. Add food colouring. Mix well. Makes 1/4 cup (60 mL) glaze. Spoon glaze into small resealable freezer bag, then snip tiny piece off corner. Drizzle glaze in decorative pattern over cookies. Let stand until set. Makes about 5 dozen (60) cookies.

1 cookie: 70 Calories; 3.5 g Total Fat (2.2 g Mono, 0.4 g Poly, 0.7 g Sat); 7 mg Cholesterol; 9 g Carbohydrate; trace Fibre; 1 g Protein; 53 mg Sodium

Pictured on page 37.

Left: Chocolate-Dipped Lemon Cookies, this page
Right: Lemon Icebox Cookies, above

Fill your kitchen with the enticing aroma of cinnamon. It's an irresistible invitation to come and taste these pretty cookies!

about cinnamon

Cinnamon comes from the inner bark of a tropical evergreen tree. As the bark dries, it twists into long, slender curls which are then cut into sticks or ground into powder. Its mild, lingering flavour is a favourite addition to cookies and other baked goods.

Cinnamon Roll Cookies

Hard margarine (or butter), softened	1 cup	250 mL
Granulated sugar	3/4 cup	175 mL
Block of cream cheese, softened	4 oz.	125 g
Large egg	1	1
Vanilla	1 tsp.	5 mL
All-purpose flour	2 1/4 cups	550 mL
Baking soda	1/2 tsp.	2 mL
Salt	1/4 tsp.	1 mL
Hard margarine (or butter), melted	1 tbsp.	15 mL
Brown sugar, packed	2 tbsp.	30 mL
Ground cinnamon	1/2 tsp.	2 mL

Cream first amount of margarine and granulated sugar in large bowl. Add cream cheese. Beat until well combined. Add egg and vanilla. Beat until smooth.

Combine flour, baking soda and salt in medium bowl. Add to margarine mixture in 2 additions, mixing well after each addition until no dry flour remains. Roll out dough between 2 sheets of waxed paper to 9 x 13 inch (22 x 33 cm) rectangle. Discard top sheet of waxed paper.

Brush second amount of margarine evenly on dough. Sprinkle brown sugar evenly over margarine. Sprinkle cinnamon evenly over top. Roll up tightly from long side, jelly roll-style, using waxed paper as a guide. Wrap with same sheet of waxed paper. Chill for at least 6 hours or overnight. Discard waxed paper. Cut into 1/4 inch (6 mm) slices. Arrange about 2 inches (5 cm) apart on greased cookie sheets. Bake in 350°F (175°C) oven for 10 to 12 minutes until golden. Let stand on cookie sheets for 5 minutes before removing to wire racks to cool. Makes about 4 dozen (48) cookies.

1 roll: 87 Calories; 5.3 g Total Fat (3.1 g Mono, 0.5 g Poly, 1.5 g Sat); 7 mg Cholesterol; 9 g Carbohydrate; trace Fibre; 1 g Protein; 85 mg Sodium

Pictured on page 39.

Lovely for lemon lovers.
Perfect for parties.

Lemon Cookies

Hard margarine (or butter), softened	1/2 cup	125 mL
Granulated sugar	1/2 cup	125 mL
Large egg	1	1
Sweetened condensed milk	2/3 cup	150 mL
Lemon juice	2 tbsp.	30 mL
Grated lemon zest	1 tbsp.	15 mL
Vanilla	1 tsp.	5 mL
All-purpose flour	2 1/4 cups	550 mL
Baking powder	2 tsp.	10 mL
Salt	1/2 tsp.	2 mL
LEMON GLAZE		
Icing (confectioner's) sugar	3/4 cup	175 mL
Water	2 tsp.	10 mL
Lemon juice	1 1/2 tsp.	7 mL

Gold or silver dragées (optional)

Cream margarine and sugar in large bowl. Add egg. Beat well. Add next 4 ingredients. Beat until smooth.

Combine flour, baking powder and salt in medium bowl. Add to margarine mixture in 2 additions, mixing well after each addition until no dry flour remains. Divide dough into 2 equal portions. Roll out 1 portion on lightly floured surface to 1/4 inch (6 mm) thickness. Cut out shapes with lightly floured 2 inch (5 cm) cookie cutter. Roll out scraps to cut more shapes. Arrange about 2 inches (5 cm) apart on greased cookie sheets. Bake in 350°F (175°C) oven for about 8 minutes until golden. Let stand on cookie sheets for 5 minutes before removing to wire racks to cool completely. Cool cookie sheets between batches. Repeat with remaining dough portion.

Lemon Glaze: Combine icing sugar, water and lemon juice in small bowl, adding more icing sugar or water if necessary until pourable consistency. Makes about 1/3 cup (75 mL) glaze. Brush glaze with small pastry brush on cookies.

Decorate with dragées. Let stand until set. Makes about 6 dozen (72) cookies.

1 cookie: 49 Calories; 1.7 g Total Fat (1 g Mono, 0.2 g Poly, 0.5 g Sat); 4 mg Cholesterol; 8 g Carbohydrate; trace Fibre; 1 g Protein; 47 mg Sodium

Pictured on page 41.

These pretty cookies are so nice, someone thought to name them twice!

tip

To avoid over-handling, roll out cookie dough between 2 sheets of waxed or parchment paper. Over-handled dough will become tough and dry.

an added touch

Cut out centres with shaped cookie cutter appropriate for the occasion. For example, use a star or tree cookie cutter for Christmas, or a heart cookie cutter for Valentine's Day.

Jam Jams

Hard margarine (or butter), softened	1 cup	250 mL
Brown sugar, packed	1/4 cup	60 mL
Granulated sugar	1/4 cup	60 mL
Large eggs	2	2
Golden corn syrup	1/2 cup	125 mL
Vanilla	1 tsp.	5 mL
All-purpose flour	3 cups	750 mL
Baking powder	1/2 tsp.	2 mL
Salt	1/2 tsp.	2 mL
Apricot or raspberry jam (or jelly), approximately	3 tbsp.	50 mL
Icing (confectioner's) sugar, for dusting		

Cream margarine and both sugars in large bowl. Add eggs 1 at a time, beating well after each addition. Add corn syrup and vanilla. Beat until smooth.

Combine flour, baking powder and salt in medium bowl. Add to margarine mixture in 3 additions, mixing well after each addition until no dry flour remains. Roll out dough on lightly floured surface to 1/8 inch (3 mm) thickness. Cut out circles with lightly floured 2 1/2 inch (6.4 cm) round cookie cutter with fluted edge. Roll out scraps to cut more circles. Arrange about 2 inches (5 cm) apart on greased cookie sheets. Cut out centres of 1/2 of circles with lightly floured 1 inch (2.5 cm) cookie cutter. Bake in 350°F (175°C) oven for 8 to 10 minutes until golden. Let stand on cookie sheets for 5 minutes before removing to wire racks to cool completely.

Spread about 1/2 tsp. (2 mL) jam on bottom of each whole cookie. Place cookies with cut-out centres on top of jam. Dust with icing sugar. Makes about 1 1/2 dozen (18) jam jams.

1 jam jam: 244 Calories; 11.5 g Total Fat (7.2 g Mono, 1.2 g Poly, 2.4 g Sat); 24 mg Cholesterol; 33 g Carbohydrate; 1 g Fibre; 3 g Protein; 224 mg Sodium

Pictured on pages 3 and 43.

Sweet coconut macaroon topping on a pastry-like base. An interesting, delicious cookie!

about coconut

Such a lovely bunch of coconut! Fine or medium, flake or shredded (long thread), unsweetened or sweetened. Be sure to pay careful attention to which type the recipe requires as each provides a slightly different texture or sweetness.

Coconut Cookies

All-purpose flour	1 cup	250 mL
Baking powder	1/2 tsp.	2 mL
Salt	1/4 tsp.	1 mL
Hard margarine (or butter), softened	1/2 cup	125 mL
Egg yolks (large)	3	3
Milk	1 tbsp.	15 mL
COCONUT TOPPING		
Egg whites (large), room temperature	3	3
Icing (confectioner's) sugar	1 1/2 cups	375 mL
Shredded (long thread) coconut	2 1/2 cups	625 mL
Hard margarine (or butter), melted	1 tbsp.	15 mL

Combine flour, baking powder and salt in medium bowl. Cut in margarine until mixture resembles fine crumbs.

Beat egg yolks and milk with fork in small cup until well combined. Slowly add to flour mixture, stirring with fork until mixture starts to come together. Do not overmix. Form into flattened disk. Roll out dough on lightly floured surface to 1/4 inch (6 mm) thickness. Cut out circles with lightly floured 2 inch (5 cm) round cookie cutter with fluted edge. Roll out scraps to cut more circles. Arrange about 2 inches (5 cm) apart on ungreased cookie sheets.

Coconut Topping: Beat egg whites in large bowl until stiff peaks form. Add icing sugar in 2 additions, beating after each addition until smooth and glossy.

Fold in coconut and margarine. Makes about 1 1/2 cups (375 mL) topping. Spoon about 2 tsp. (10 mL) topping on top of each circle. Bake in 300°F (150°C) oven for about 30 minutes until golden. Remove to wire racks to cool. Makes about 2 1/2 dozen (30) cookies.

1 cookie: 133 Calories; 9.3 g Total Fat (2.8 g Mono, 0.5 g Poly, 5.4 g Sat); 22 mg Cholesterol; 12 g Carbohydrate; trace Fibre; 2 g Protein; 78 mg Sodium

Pictured on page 45.

A little cookie with your coffee—a little coffee in your cookie!

tip

To prevent hot cookies from crumbling or bending, cool them on the cookie sheet for 5 minutes before removing to a wire rack to cool completely, unless otherwise instructed.

Coffee Fingers

Hard margarine (or butter), softened	1 cup	250 mL
Brown sugar, packed	1/2 cup	125 mL
Egg yolk (large)	1	1
All-purpose flour	2 cups	500 mL
Icing (confectioner's) sugar	1/4 cup	60 mL
Instant coffee granules, crushed to fine powder	1 tsp.	5 mL
Egg white (large)	1	1
Finely chopped walnuts (or your favourite nuts)	1 1/2 cups	375 mL

Cream margarine and brown sugar in large bowl. Add egg yolk. Beat well.

Combine flour, icing sugar and crushed coffee granules in medium bowl. Add to margarine mixture in 2 additions, mixing well after each addition until no dry flour remains. Divide dough into 2 equal portions. Shape each portion into 6 inch (15 cm) long log. Roll out 1 log on lightly floured surface to 4 x 6 inch (10 x 15 cm) rectangle, about 1/2 inch (12 mm) thick. Cut into 1/2 x 2 inch (1.2 x 5 cm) rectangles.

Fork-beat egg white in small bowl.

Put walnuts into separate small bowl. Dip each rectangle in egg white until coated. Roll each in walnuts until coated, shaping into finger as you roll. Arrange about 2 inches (5 cm) apart on greased cookie sheets. Bake in 300°F (150°C) oven for 20 to 25 minutes until golden. Let stand on cookie sheets for 5 minutes before removing to wire racks to cool. Repeat with remaining log, egg white and walnuts. Makes about 4 dozen (48) fingers.

1 finger: 94 Calories; 6.5 g Total Fat (3.2 g Mono, 2 g Poly, 1 g Sat); 4 mg Cholesterol; 8 g Carbohydrate; trace Fibre; 2 g Protein; 50 mg Sodium

Pictured on page 47.

Get your fill of raisins with these scrumptious treats. Excellent with ice cream for dessert!

Raisin-Filled Cookies

RAISIN FILLING

Coarsely chopped raisins	1 1/4 cups	300 mL
Granulated sugar	1/2 cup	125 mL
Water	1/2 cup	125 mL
Cornstarch	2 tsp.	10 mL
Lemon juice	1 tsp.	5 mL
Hard margarine (or butter), softened	1 cup	250 mL
Granulated sugar	1 1/2 cups	375 mL
Large eggs	2	2
Vanilla	1 tsp.	5 mL
All-purpose flour	3 1/2 cups	875 mL
Baking soda	1 tsp.	5 mL
Salt	1/2 tsp.	2 mL

Granulated sugar, for decorating

Raisin Filling: Combine first 5 ingredients in medium saucepan. Bring to a boil on medium. Boil gently for 5 minutes, stirring occasionally. Remove from heat. Cool. Makes about 1 1/4 cups (300 mL) filling.

Cream margarine and second amount of sugar in large bowl. Add eggs 1 at a time, beating well after each addition. Add vanilla. Beat until smooth.

Combine flour, baking soda and salt in medium bowl. Add to margarine mixture in 3 additions, mixing well after each addition until no dry flour remains. Divide dough into 2 equal portions. Roll out 1 portion on lightly floured surface to 1/4 inch (6 mm) thickness. Cut out circles with lightly floured 2 1/2 inch (6.4 cm) round cookie cutter. Roll out scraps to cut more circles. Spread about 1 tsp. (5 mL) filling evenly on 1/2 of circles, leaving 1/4 inch (6 mm) edge. Place remaining circles on top of filling. Press edges together with fork to seal. Arrange about 2 inches (5 cm) apart on greased cookie sheets. Carefully cut 1/2 inch (12 mm) X in top of each cookie.

Sprinkle each cookie with third amount of sugar. Bake in 350°F (175°C) oven for about 10 minutes until golden. Let stand on cookie sheets for 5 minutes before removing to wire racks to cool. Repeat with remaining dough portion, filling and sugar. Makes about 3 dozen (36) cookies.

1 cookie: 161 Calories; 5.8 g Total Fat (3.6 g Mono, 0.6 g Poly, 1.2 g Sat); 12 mg Cholesterol; 26 g Carbohydrate; trace Fibre; 2 g Protein; 136 mg Sodium

Pictured on page 49.

Little pastry envelopes stuffed with a delightful filling.

pretty presentation

To create a visually impressive sweet tray, use varied shapes of cookies such as square, round or cut-out. For best eye-appeal, keep the cookies about the same size. Arrange them diagonally on the tray and choose a different shape for each row.

Sour Cream Nut Rolls

ALMOND FILLING

Ground almonds	2 1/2 cups	625 mL
Granulated sugar	1/2 cup	125 mL
Milk	1/4 cup	60 mL
Almond flavouring	1 tsp.	5 mL
All-purpose flour	2 cups	500 mL
Hard margarine (or butter), softened	1 cup	250 mL
Egg yolks (large)	2	2
Sour cream	1/2 cup	125 mL

Almond Filling: Combine first 4 ingredients in medium bowl. Makes 2 cups (500 mL) filling.

Measure flour into large bowl. Cut in margarine until mixture resembles fine crumbs.

Beat egg yolks and sour cream with whisk in small bowl until well combined. Slowly add to flour mixture, stirring with fork until mixture starts to come together. Do not overmix. Divide dough into 2 equal portions. Shape each portion into 6 inch (15 cm) long log. Flatten slightly. Roll out 1 log on lightly floured surface to 12 x 16 inch (30 x 40 cm) rectangle. Cut into 2 inch (5 cm) squares. Spoon about 1 tsp. (5 mL) filling across centre of each square. Fold diagonally opposite corners over filling. Pinch together to seal. Arrange about 2 inches (5 cm) apart on ungreased cookie sheets. Bake in 350°F (175°C) oven for 10 to 12 minutes until golden. Let stand on cookie sheets for 5 minutes before removing to wire racks to cool. Repeat with remaining log and filling. Makes about 8 dozen (96) rolls.

1 roll: *46 Calories; 3.3 g Total Fat (2 g Mono, 0.4 g Poly, 0.7 g Sat); 5 mg Cholesterol; 4 g Carbohydrate; trace Fibre; 1 g Protein; 25 mg Sodium*

Pictured on page 51.

Lovely chocolate cookies sandwich a delectable chocolate filling accented with bourbon. Perfect for tea time.

variation

To make these cookies child-friendly, prepare the filling with 1 tsp. (5 mL) rum or brandy flavouring plus 2 tsp. (10 mL) water instead of using bourbon.

Bourbon Cookies

Hard margarine (or butter), softened	6 tbsp.	100 mL
Granulated sugar	1/4 cup	60 mL
Large egg	1	1
Golden corn syrup	2 tbsp.	30 mL
All-purpose flour	1 1/2 cups	375 mL
Cocoa, sifted if lumpy	1/4 cup	60 mL
Granulated sugar, for decorating		
BOURBON FILLING		
Semi-sweet chocolate chips	1/3 cup	75 mL
Bourbon whisky	1 tbsp.	15 mL
Icing (confectioner's) sugar	1 cup	250 mL
Hard margarine (or butter), softened	1/2 cup	125 mL

Cream margarine and first amount of granulated sugar in large bowl. Add egg. Beat well. Add corn syrup. Beat until smooth.

Combine flour and cocoa in small bowl. Add to margarine mixture in 2 additions, mixing well after each addition until no dry flour remains. Divide dough into 2 equal portions. Shape each portion into 6 inch (15 cm) long log. Flatten slightly. Roll out 1 log on lightly floured surface to 9 x 10 inch (22 x 25 cm) rectangle. Cut into 1 x 3 inch (2.5 x 7.5 cm) rectangles. Arrange about 2 inches (5 cm) apart on greased cookie sheets. Bake in 350°F (175°C) oven for 10 to 15 minutes until firm. Remove from oven.

Immediately sprinkle with second amount of granulated sugar. Let stand on cookie sheets for 5 minutes before removing to wire racks to cool completely. Repeat with remaining log and granulated sugar.

Bourbon Filling: Heat chocolate chips in small heavy saucepan on lowest heat, stirring often until almost melted. Do not overheat. Remove from heat. Stir until smooth. Cool to room temperature. Add bourbon. Stir.

Beat icing sugar and margarine in medium bowl until smooth. Add chocolate mixture. Beat well. Makes about 1 cup (250 mL) filling. Spread about 1/2 tbsp. (7 mL) filling on bottom of 1/2 of cookies. Place remaining cookies, sugar-side up, on top of filling. Makes about 2 1/2 dozen (30) cookies.

1 cookie: 115 Calories; 6.5 g Total Fat (3.9 g Mono, 0.6 g Poly, 1.6 g Sat); 7 mg Cholesterol; 14 g Carbohydrate; 1 g Fibre; 1 g Protein; 69 mg Sodium

Pictured on page 53.

These soft, old-fashioned cookies are a comforting snack. Great with a glass of milk any time!

Thick Molasses Cookies

Granulated sugar	1 cup	250 mL
Cooking oil	1 cup	250 mL
Large egg	1	1
Fancy (mild) molasses	1 cup	250 mL
Milk	1/2 cup	125 mL
Baking soda	2 tsp.	10 mL
All-purpose flour	5 1/2 cups	1.4 L
Salt	1/2 tsp.	2 mL

Beat sugar, cooking oil and egg in large bowl until thick and pale. Add molasses. Beat well.

Stir milk into baking soda in small cup until dissolved. Add to molasses mixture. Beat until smooth.

Combine flour and salt in separate large bowl. Add to molasses mixture in 3 additions, mixing well after each addition until no dry flour remains. Divide dough into 2 equal portions. Roll out 1 portion on lightly floured surface to 1/4 inch (6 mm) thickness. Cut out circles with lightly floured 2 1/2 inch (6.4 cm) round cookie cutter with fluted edge. Roll out scraps to cut more circles. Arrange about 2 inches (5 cm) apart on greased cookie sheets. Bake in 375°F (190°C) oven for 8 to 10 minutes until firm. Let stand on cookie sheets for 5 minutes before removing to wire racks to cool. Repeat with remaining dough portion. Makes about 5 dozen (60) cookies.

1 cookie: 109 Calories; 4.1 g Total Fat (2.3 g Mono, 1.2 g Poly, 0.3 g Sat); 4 mg Cholesterol; 17 g Carbohydrate; trace Fibre; 1 g Protein; 67 mg Sodium

Pictured on page 55.

Send them a kiss in their lunch boxes. Chocolate centres make these awesome blossoms look a bit like flowers.

Peanut Blossoms

Hard margarine (or butter), softened	1/2 cup	125 mL
Brown sugar, packed	1/2 cup	125 mL
Granulated sugar	1/2 cup	125 mL
Smooth peanut butter	1/2 cup	125 mL
Large egg	1	1
Milk	2 tbsp.	30 mL
Vanilla	1 tsp.	5 mL
All-purpose flour	1 3/4 cups	425 mL
Baking soda	1 tsp.	5 mL
Salt	1/2 tsp.	2 mL
Granulated sugar, approximately	1/3 cup	75 mL
Milk chocolate kisses, approximately	54	54

Cream margarine, brown sugar and first amount of granulated sugar in large bowl. Add peanut butter. Beat until well combined.

Add egg, milk and vanilla. Beat until smooth.

Combine flour, baking soda and salt in small bowl. Add to peanut butter mixture in 2 additions, mixing well after each addition until no dry flour remains. Roll into 1 inch (2.5 cm) balls.

Roll each ball in second amount of granulated sugar in same small bowl until coated. Arrange about 2 inches (5 cm) apart on ungreased cookie sheets. Bake in 375°F (190°C) oven for about 10 minutes until golden. Remove from oven.

Immediately place 1 chocolate kiss on top of each cookie. Press down until cookie cracks around edge. Let stand on cookie sheets for 5 minutes before removing to wire racks to cool. Makes about 4 1/2 dozen (54) cookies.

1 cookie: 90 Calories; 4.4 g Total Fat (2.2 g Mono, 0.6 g Poly, 1.4 g Sat); 5 mg Cholesterol; 12 g Carbohydrate; trace Fibre; 2 g Protein; 84 mg Sodium

Pictured on page 57.

With no flour and only three ingredients, the name pretty much says it all.

Easy Peanut Butter Cookies

Large egg	1	1
Granulated sugar	1 cup	250 mL
Crunchy peanut butter	1 cup	250 mL

Beat egg and sugar in medium bowl until thick and pale.

Add peanut butter. Beat until smooth. Cover. Chill for 1 hour. Roll into balls, using 1 tbsp. (15 mL) dough for each. Arrange about 2 inches (5 cm) apart on greased cookie sheets. Bake in 350°F (175°C) oven for 12 to 14 minutes until golden. Let stand on cookie sheets for 5 minutes before removing to wire racks to cool. Makes about 2 dozen (24) cookies.

1 cookie: 104 Calories; 5.9 g Total Fat (2.8 g Mono, 1.7 g Poly, 1.2 g Sat); 9 mg Cholesterol; 11 g Carbohydrate; 1 g Fibre; 3 g Protein; 58 mg Sodium

Pictured on page 59.

Delightfully decadent! Cranberries and white chocolate are a perfect pair.

Cranberry White Chocolate Cookies

Large eggs	2	2
Brown sugar, packed	1 3/4 cups	425 mL
Cooking oil	1/2 cup	125 mL
Vanilla	1 tsp.	5 mL
All-purpose flour	1 3/4 cups	425 mL
Baking powder	1 tsp.	5 mL
Baking soda	1/2 tsp.	2 mL
Dried cranberries	1 cup	250 mL
White chocolate chips	1 cup	250 mL

Beat eggs and brown sugar in large bowl until thick and pale. Add cooking oil and vanilla. Beat until smooth.

Combine next 3 ingredients in small bowl. Add to brown sugar mixture in 2 additions, mixing well after each addition until no dry flour remains.

(continued on next page)

Add cranberries and white chocolate chips. Mix well. Cover. Chill for 1 hour. Roll into balls, using 1 tbsp. (15 mL) dough for each. Arrange about 2 inches (5 cm) apart on greased cookie sheets. Bake in 375°F (190°C) oven for about 10 minutes until golden. Let stand on cookie sheets for 5 minutes before removing to wire racks to cool. Makes about 4 dozen (48) cookies.

1 cookie: 98 Calories; 3.8 g Total Fat (1.9 g Mono, 0.8 g Poly, 0.9 g Sat); 10 mg Cholesterol; 15 g Carbohydrate; 1 g Fibre; 1 g Protein; 31 mg Sodium

Pictured below.

Left: Easy Peanut Butter Cookies, page 58
Right: Cranberry White Chocolate Cookies, page 58

Kids will love these chocolatey treats. Perfect party fare.

Dirt Cups

COOKIE CUPS

Hard margarine (or butter), softened	1/4 cup	60 mL
Granulated sugar	1/2 cup	125 mL
Large egg	1	1
Vanilla	1/4 tsp.	1 mL
All-purpose flour	1 cup	250 mL
Cocoa, sifted if lumpy	3 tbsp.	50 mL
Salt	1/8 tsp.	0.5 mL

DIRT FILLING

Box of instant chocolate pudding powder (4 serving size)	1	1
Cold milk	1 cup	250 mL
Light sour cream	1/2 cup	125 mL
Gummy worms	24	24
Chocolate wafer crumbs	1/2 cup	125 mL

Cookie Cups: Cream margarine and sugar in medium bowl. Add egg and vanilla. Beat until smooth.

Combine flour, cocoa and salt in small bowl. Add to margarine mixture. Mix until no dry flour remains. Divide dough into 24 equal portions. Roll into balls. Press each ball into bottom and up side of greased mini-muffin cup. Bake in 350°F (175°C) oven for 8 to 10 minutes until firm. Let stand in pans on wire racks to cool slightly. Run knife around inside edge of each muffin cup to loosen. Remove cookie shells to wire racks to cool completely.

Dirt Filling: Beat pudding powder, cold milk and sour cream in separate medium bowl for about 1 minute until smooth. Makes about 2 cups (500 mL) filling. Spoon into each cookie shell.

Insert 1 gummy worm partway into filling in each shell. Sprinkle wafer crumbs over filling. Makes about 2 dozen (24) dirt cups.

1 dirt cup: 126 Calories; 3.3 g Total Fat (1.9 g Mono, 0.4 g Poly, 1.2 g Sat); 11 mg Cholesterol; 23 g Carbohydrate; trace Fibre; 2 g Protein; 129 mg Sodium

Pictured on page 61.

Top right: Dirt Cups, above
Bottom left: Egg Nests, page 62

Great any time, but especially cute for Easter.

Egg Nests

Oriental steam-fried noodles, broken up	3 cups	750 mL
Semi-sweet chocolate chips	1 cup	250 mL
Butterscotch (or peanut butter) chips	1 cup	250 mL
Jelly beans (your favourite), approximately	50	50

Measure noodles into large bowl.

Heat both chocolate and butterscotch chips in small heavy saucepan on lowest heat, stirring often until almost melted. Do not overheat. Remove from heat. Stir until smooth. Add to noodles. Stir until coated. Drop, using 1/3 cup (75 mL) for each, onto waxed paper-lined cookie sheets. Dent each in centre with thumb. Let stand until set. May be chilled to speed setting.

Put 5 jelly beans into each dent. Makes about 10 egg nests.

1 egg nest: 271 Calories; 10.3 g Total Fat (2.9 g Mono, 2.7 g Poly, 3.9 g Sat); 1 mg Cholesterol; 47 g Carbohydrate; 2 g Fibre; 2 g Protein; 74 mg Sodium

Pictured on page 61.

A spicy cookie made for dunking.

about ginger

Ground ginger is a hot, sweet spice derived from gingerroot. It is commonly used in Western cuisine to spice cakes and cookies. Gingerroot is more typically used in Asian cooking, and is not a substitute for ground ginger in baking.

Gingersnaps

Hard margarine (or butter), softened	3/4 cup	175 mL
Granulated sugar	1 cup	250 mL
Large egg	1	1
Fancy (mild) molasses	1/2 cup	125 mL
All-purpose flour	2 1/2 cups	625 mL
Baking soda	2 tsp.	10 mL
Ground ginger	2 tsp.	10 mL
Ground cinnamon	1 tsp.	5 mL
Salt	1/2 tsp.	2 mL
Granulated sugar, approximately	1/4 cup	60 mL

Cream margarine and first amount of sugar in large bowl. Add egg. Beat well. Add molasses. Beat until smooth.

(continued on next page)

Combine next 5 ingredients in medium bowl. Add to margarine mixture in 2 additions, mixing well after each addition until no dry flour remains. Roll into 1 inch (2.5 cm) balls.

Roll each ball in second amount of sugar in small bowl until coated. Arrange about 2 inches (5 cm) apart on greased cookie sheets. Bake in 350°F (175°C) oven for about 10 minutes until just firm. Let stand on cookie sheets for about 5 minutes before removing to wire racks to cool. Makes about 7 1/2 dozen (90) cookies.

1 cookie: 45 Calories; 1.7 g Total Fat (1.1 g Mono, 0.2 g Poly, 0.4 g Sat); 2 mg Cholesterol; 7 g Carbohydrate; trace Fibre; 0 g Protein; 62 mg Sodium

Pictured below.

These pretty Crinkles make their eyes twinkle with delight!

Chocolate Crinkles

Hard margarine (or butter), softened	1/4 cup	60 mL
Granulated sugar	2 cups	500 mL
Large eggs	3	3
Vanilla	2 tsp.	10 mL
Unsweetened chocolate baking squares (1 oz., 28 g, each), chopped	4	4
All-purpose flour	2 1/2 cups	625 mL
Baking powder	2 tsp.	10 mL
Salt	1/2 tsp.	2 mL
Icing (confectioner's) sugar, approximately	1 cup	250 mL

Cream margarine and granulated sugar in large bowl. Add eggs 1 at a time, beating well after each addition. Add vanilla. Beat until smooth.

Heat chocolate in small heavy saucepan on lowest heat, stirring often until almost melted. Do not overheat. Remove from heat. Stir until smooth. Add to margarine mixture. Beat well.

Combine flour, baking powder and salt in medium bowl. Add to chocolate mixture in 2 additions, mixing well after each addition until no dry flour remains. Roll into 1 inch (2.5 cm) balls.

Roll each ball in icing sugar in small bowl until coated. Arrange about 2 inches (5 cm) apart on greased cookie sheets. Bake in 350°F (175°C) oven for 10 minutes. Cookies will be soft. Let stand on cookie sheets for 5 minutes before removing to wire racks to cool. Makes about 8 dozen (96) cookies.

1 cookie: 48 Calories; 1.4 g Total Fat (0.6 g Mono, 0.1 g Poly, 0.5 g Sat); 7 mg Cholesterol; 9 g Carbohydrate; trace Fibre; 1 g Protein; 28 mg Sodium

Pictured on page 65.

Crisp, chocolate biscotti dotted with chewy cranberries. Dunk away!

about biscotti

Biscotti is an Italian term meaning "twice baked." The dough is first baked as a loaf, then sliced and baked again to become hard and crunchy. Biscotti is great dipped into coffee or tea, and makes an excellent gift.

Choco-Cran Biscotti

Dried cranberries	1 cup	250 mL
Orange juice	3 tbsp.	50 mL
All-purpose flour	2 cups	500 mL
Cocoa, sifted if lumpy	1/3 cup	75 mL
Baking powder	1 tsp.	5 mL
Salt	1/4 tsp.	1 mL
Hard margarine (or butter), softened	1/4 cup	60 mL
Granulated sugar	1/2 cup	125 mL
Large eggs	3	3

Combine cranberries and orange juice in small microwave-safe bowl. Cover. Microwave on high (100%) for about 1 minute, rotating dish at halftime if microwave does not have turntable, until cranberries are softened. Cool.

Combine next 4 ingredients in large bowl. Make a well in centre.

Cream margarine and sugar in medium bowl. Add eggs 1 at a time, beating well after each addition. Add cranberry mixture. Stir. Add to well. Mix until soft dough forms. Turn out onto lightly floured surface. Knead 6 times. Shape into 16 inch (40 cm) long log. Place on greased cookie sheet. Flatten slightly. Bake in 350°F (175°C) oven for 30 minutes. Let stand on cookie sheet for 10 to 15 minutes until cool enough to handle. Cut log diagonally with serrated knife into 1/2 inch (12 mm) slices. Arrange, cut-side down, about 2 inches (5 cm) apart on same cookie sheet. Bake in 275°F (140°C) oven for 10 to 12 minutes until golden. Turn slices over. Turn oven off. Let stand in oven for another 30 minutes until dry and crisp. Remove to wire racks to cool. Makes about 2 dozen (24) biscotti.

1 biscotti: 97 Calories; 3 g Total Fat (1.6 g Mono, 0.3 g Poly, 0.7 g Sat); 27 mg Cholesterol; 16 g Carbohydrate; 1 g Fibre; 2 g Protein; 73 mg Sodium

Pictured on page 68.

Nutty Biscotti

All-purpose flour	2 1/2 cups	625 mL
Flaked hazelnuts (filberts), toasted (see Note)	2/3 cup	150 mL
Baking soda	1 tsp.	5 mL
Salt	1/4 tsp.	1 mL
Hard margarine (or butter), softened	1/4 cup	60 mL
Granulated sugar	3/4 cup	175 mL
Large eggs	2	2
Egg white (large)	1	1
Hazelnut-flavoured liqueur (such as Frangelico), optional	1 tbsp.	15 mL
Vanilla	1 tsp.	5 mL

Combine first 4 ingredients in large bowl. Make a well in centre.

Cream margarine and sugar in medium bowl. Add eggs 1 at a time, beating well after each addition. Add egg white. Beat well.

Add liqueur and vanilla. Beat until smooth. Add to well. Mix until soft dough forms. Turn out onto lightly floured surface. Knead 6 times. Shape into 16 inch (40 cm) long log. Place on greased cookie sheet. Flatten slightly. Bake in 350°F (175°C) oven for about 30 minutes until golden. Let stand on cookie sheet for 10 to 15 minutes until cool enough to handle. Cut log diagonally with serrated knife into 1/2 inch (12 mm) slices. Arrange, cut-side down, about 2 inches (5 cm) apart on same cookie sheet. Bake in 275°F (140°C) oven for 10 to 12 minutes until golden. Turn slices over. Turn oven off. Let stand in oven for about 30 minutes until dry and crisp. Remove to wire racks to cool. Makes about 2 dozen (24) biscotti.

1 biscotti: 123 Calories; 4.7 g Total Fat (3.2 g Mono, 0.5 g Poly, 0.7 g Sat); 18 mg Cholesterol; 18 g Carbohydrate; 1 g Fibre; 3 g Protein; 110 mg Sodium

Pictured on page 69.

Keep these in a clear glass cookie jar beside your coffee maker. Then there will always be something ready to serve when a friend drops by for coffee.

note

To toast nuts, spread them evenly in an ungreased shallow pan. Bake in a 350°F (175°C) oven for 5 to 10 minutes, stirring or shaking often, until desired doneness.

chocolate-dipped nutty biscotti

Heat 3/4 cup (175 mL) semi-sweet chocolate chips in small heavy saucepan on lowest heat, stirring often until almost melted. Do not overheat. Remove from heat. Stir until smooth. Hold biscotti by the end and dip straight down into chocolate until 1 inch (2.5 cm) is coated. Place on waxed paper-lined cookie sheet. Let stand until set.

Pictured on page 69.

Photo legend, next page
(Clockwise from left)
Filbert Fingers, page 71
Choco-Cran Biscotti, page 66
Snickerdoodles, page 70
Chocolate-Dipped Nutty Biscotti, above
Nutty Biscotti, this page
Snickerdoodles, page 70

An old favourite. Simple cinnamon flavour makes them irresistible.

Snickerdoodles

Hard margarine (or butter), softened	1 cup	250 mL
Granulated sugar	1 1/2 cups	375 mL
Large eggs	2	2
All-purpose flour	2 1/2 cups	625 mL
Cream of tartar	2 tsp.	10 mL
Baking soda	1 tsp.	5 mL
Salt	1/4 tsp.	1 mL
Granulated sugar	2 tbsp.	30 mL
Ground cinnamon	2 tsp.	10 mL

Cream margarine and first amount of sugar in large bowl. Add eggs 1 at a time, beating well after each addition.

Combine next 4 ingredients in medium bowl. Add to margarine mixture in 2 additions, mixing well after each addition until no dry flour remains. Roll into 1 inch (2.5 cm) balls.

Combine second amount of sugar and cinnamon in small bowl. Roll each ball in cinnamon mixture until coated. Arrange about 2 inches (5 cm) apart on ungreased cookie sheets. Bake in 375°F (190°C) oven for about 10 minutes until golden. Let stand on cookie sheets for 5 minutes before removing to wire racks to cool. Makes about 4 1/2 dozen (54) cookies.

1 cookie: 82 Calories; 3.8 g Total Fat (2.4 g Mono, 0.4 g Poly, 0.8 g Sat); 8 mg Cholesterol; 11 g Carbohydrate; trace Fibre; 1 g Protein; 79 mg Sodium

Pictured on pages 68/69.

Filbert Fingers

Butter (not margarine), softened	1 cup	250 mL
Brown sugar, packed	3/4 cup	175 mL
Milk	2 tbsp.	30 mL
All-purpose flour	2 1/2 cups	625 mL
Ground hazelnuts (filberts)	1 cup	250 mL
Semi-sweet chocolate melting wafers	1/3 cup	75 mL

Cream butter and brown sugar in large bowl. Add milk. Beat until smooth.

Add flour in 2 additions, mixing well after each addition until no dry flour remains. Add hazelnuts. Mix well. Shape into 2 inch (5 cm) long logs, using 1 tbsp. (15 mL) dough for each. Arrange about 2 inches (5 cm) apart on ungreased cookie sheets. Bake in 375°F (190°C) oven for about 10 minutes until golden. Let stand on cookie sheets for 5 minutes before removing to wire racks to cool completely.

Heat chocolate wafers in small heavy saucepan on lowest heat, stirring often until almost melted. Do not overheat. Remove from heat. Stir until smooth. Transfer to small custard cup. Holding the centre of 1 log, dip 1/2 inch (12 mm) of 1 end straight down into chocolate. Repeat with opposite end. Place on waxed paper-lined cookie sheet. Repeat with remaining logs and chocolate. Let stand until set. May be chilled to speed setting. Makes about 4 dozen (48) fingers.

1 finger: 91 Calories; 5.5 g Total Fat (2.1 g Mono, 0.3 g Poly, 2.8 g Sat); 11 mg Cholesterol; 10 g Carbohydrate; trace Fibre; 1 g Protein; 43 mg Sodium

Pictured on page 68.

Fabulous hazelnut cookies to share with family and friends.

tip

An alternative to melting chocolate on the stovetop is to melt it in the microwave. Heat the chocolate in a small, uncovered microwave-safe bowl on medium-high (70%) for 30 seconds. Stir well. Repeat heating and stirring until chocolate is smooth and glossy. Never put a lid on melting chocolate. Condensation can develop and the water will cause the chocolate to seize.

A pretty thimble cookie with an inviting cherry centre.

Cherry Winks

Hard margarine (or butter), softened	3/4 cup	175 mL
Granulated sugar	1 cup	250 mL
Large eggs	2	2
All-purpose flour	2 cups	500 mL
Baking powder	1 tsp.	5 mL
Baking soda	1/2 tsp.	2 mL
Salt	1/2 tsp.	2 mL
Chopped pecans (or walnuts)	1 cup	250 mL
Chopped pitted dates (or raisins)	1 cup	250 mL
Cornflake crumbs	3 cups	750 mL
Maraschino cherries, halved and blotted dry, approximately	42	42

Cream margarine and sugar in large bowl. Add eggs 1 at a time, beating well after each addition.

Combine next 4 ingredients in medium bowl. Add to margarine mixture in 2 additions, mixing well after each addition until no dry flour remains.

Add pecans and dates. Mix well. Roll into 1 inch (2.5 cm) balls.

Roll each ball in cornflake crumbs in separate medium bowl until coated. Arrange about 2 inches (5 cm) apart on greased cookie sheets. Dent each with thumb. Place 1 cherry half in each dent. Press down lightly. Bake in 350°F (175°C) oven for 10 to 12 minutes until golden. Let stand on cookie sheets for 5 minutes before removing to wire racks to cool. Makes about 7 dozen (84) cookies.

1 cookie: 71 Calories; 2.9 g Total Fat (1.8 g Mono, 0.5 g Poly, 0.5 g Sat); 5 mg Cholesterol; 11 g Carbohydrate; 1 g Fibre; 1 g Protein; 83 mg Sodium

Pictured on page 73.

Golden cookies with refreshing lemon flavour. Perfect with a cup of tea.

tip

When a recipe calls for both lemon zest and juice, grate the lemon first, then juice it.

variation

Add 1 cup (250 mL) raisins to the dough. Mix well. Roll into balls and bake as directed.

Lemon Crackles

Hard margarine (or butter), softened	1/2 cup	125 mL
Brown sugar, packed	1/2 cup	125 mL
Granulated sugar	1/4 cup	60 mL
Large egg	1	1
Lemon juice	2 tbsp.	30 mL
Grated lemon zest	1 tbsp.	15 mL
All-purpose flour	1 1/2 cups	375 mL
Baking powder	1 tsp.	5 mL
Baking soda	1/2 tsp.	2 mL
Granulated sugar, approximately	1/4 cup	60 mL

Cream margarine, brown sugar and first amount of granulated sugar in large bowl. Add egg. Beat well. Add lemon juice and zest. Beat until smooth.

Combine flour, baking powder and soda in medium bowl. Add to margarine mixture in 2 additions, mixing well after each addition until no dry flour remains. Roll into 1 inch (2.5 cm) balls.

Roll each ball in second amount of granulated sugar in small bowl until coated. Arrange about 2 inches (5 cm) apart on ungreased cookie sheets. Bake in 350°F (175°C) oven for 10 to 15 minutes until golden. Let stand on cookie sheets for 5 minutes before removing to wire racks to cool. Makes about 4 dozen (48) cookies.

1 cookie: 53 Calories; 2.2 g Total Fat (1.4 g Mono, 0.2 g Poly, 0.5 g Sat); 4 mg Cholesterol; 8 g Carbohydrate; trace Fibre; 1 g Protein; 47 mg Sodium

Pictured on page 75.

Sometimes known as Mexican Wedding Cakes or Russian Tea Cakes, these make an attractive addition to a plate of sweets.

buried cherry balls

Prepare cookie dough as directed. Roll into balls. Drain and blot dry 66 maraschino cherries. Press 1 cherry into each ball. Re-roll each ball to completely cover cherry with dough. Bake as directed.

almond balls

Omit the vanilla and pecans. Use the same amounts of almond flavouring and ground almonds.

Exceptionally good—just crackerjack!

Pecan Balls

Hard margarine (or butter), softened	1 cup	250 mL
Icing (confectioner's) sugar	1/2 cup	125 mL
Vanilla	2 tsp.	10 mL
All-purpose flour	2 1/4 cups	550 mL
Ground pecans	1 cup	250 mL
Icing (confectioner's) sugar, approximately	1/2 cup	125 mL

Beat margarine, first amount of icing sugar and vanilla in large bowl until smooth.

Add flour in 2 additions, mixing well after each addition until no dry flour remains. Add pecans. Mix well. Roll into 1 inch (2.5 cm) balls. Arrange about 2 inches (5 cm) apart on ungreased cookie sheets. Bake in 325°F (160°C) oven for about 20 minutes until golden. Let stand on cookie sheets for about 5 minutes until cool enough to handle.

Roll each ball in second amount of icing sugar in small bowl until coated. Place on waxed paper-lined cookie sheets. Cool. Makes about 5 1/2 dozen (66) balls.

1 ball: 61 Calories; 4 g Total Fat (2.6 g Mono, 0.6 g Poly, 0.7 g Sat); 0 mg Cholesterol; 6 g Carbohydrate; trace Fibre; 1 g Protein; 34 mg Sodium

Pictured on page 77.

Crackerjack Cookies

Hard margarine (or butter), softened	1 cup	250 mL
Brown sugar, packed	1 cup	250 mL
Granulated sugar	1 cup	250 mL
Large eggs	2	2
Vanilla	2 tsp.	10 mL
All-purpose flour	1 1/2 cups	375 mL
Baking powder	1 tsp.	5 mL
Baking soda	1 tsp.	5 mL

(continued on next page)

Quick-cooking rolled oats (not instant)	2 cups	500 mL
Crisp rice cereal	2 cups	500 mL
Medium unsweetened coconut	1 cup	250 mL

Cream margarine and both sugars in medium bowl. Add eggs 1 at a time, beating well after each addition. Add vanilla. Beat until smooth.

Combine flour, baking powder and soda in small bowl. Add to margarine mixture in 2 additions, mixing well after each addition until no dry flour remains.

Add rolled oats, cereal and coconut. Mix well. Roll into 1 inch (2.5 cm) balls. Arrange about 2 inches (5 cm) apart on ungreased cookie sheets. Bake in 375°F (190°C) oven for 7 to 9 minutes until golden. Let stand on cookie sheets for 5 minutes before removing to wire racks to cool. Makes about 6 dozen (72) cookies.

1 cookie: 83 Calories; 3.9 g Total Fat (1.9 g Mono, 0.4 g Poly, 1.4 g Sat); 6 mg Cholesterol; 11 g Carbohydrate; trace Fibre; 1 g Protein; 66 mg Sodium

Pictured below.

Left: Crackerjack Cookies, page 76
Right: Pecan Balls, page 76

An attractive, sweet treat with a traditional flavour combination that's hard to beat!

sacher torte bites

Instead of cherries, fill each dent with apricot jam. Drizzle with chocolate as directed.

Black Forest Cookies

Hard margarine (or butter), softened	1 cup	250 mL
Box of instant chocolate pudding powder (4 serving size)	1	1
Large egg	1	1
All-purpose flour	2 cups	500 mL
Granulated sugar, approximately	1/4 cup	60 mL
Maraschino cherries, drained and blotted dry, approximately	66	66
Semi-sweet chocolate chips	1/2 cup	125 mL
Hard margarine (or butter)	3 tbsp.	50 mL

Beat first amount of margarine and pudding powder in medium bowl. Add egg. Beat well. Add flour in 2 additions, beating well after each addition until no dry flour remains. Roll into 1 inch (2.5 cm) balls.

Roll each ball in sugar in small bowl until coated. Arrange about 2 inches (5 cm) apart on greased cookie sheets. Dent each with thumb. Bake in 325°F (160°C) oven for 5 minutes. Remove from oven. Press dents again. Bake for another 10 minutes until firm. Let stand on cookie sheets for 5 minutes before removing to wire racks to cool.

Place 1 cherry in each dent.

Heat chocolate chips and second amount of margarine in small heavy saucepan on lowest heat, stirring often until chips are almost melted. Do not overheat. Remove from heat. Stir until smooth. Spoon chocolate into piping bag fitted with small writing tip or small resealable freezer bag with tiny piece snipped off corner. Drizzle small amount of chocolate mixture in decorative pattern over each cookie. Let stand until set. Makes about 5 1/2 dozen (66) cookies.

1 cookie: 70 Calories; 4 g Total Fat (2.4 g Mono, 0.4 g Poly, 1 g Sat); 3 mg Cholesterol; 8 g Carbohydrate; trace Fibre; 1 g Protein; 67 mg Sodium

Pictured on front cover and on pages 3 and 79.

Doubly delicious! Creamy filling and strawberry jam sandwiched between crisp cookies.

Strawberry Cream Cookies

Hard margarine (or butter), softened	3/4 cup	175 mL
Brown sugar, packed	1/2 cup	125 mL
Large egg	1	1
Vanilla	1/2 tsp.	2 mL
All-purpose flour	2 cups	500 mL
Baking powder	2 tsp.	10 mL
Baking soda	1/4 tsp.	1 mL
Salt	1/4 tsp.	1 mL
Medium unsweetened coconut	1/2 cup	125 mL
STRAWBERRY FILLING		
Icing (confectioner's) sugar	3/4 cup	175 mL
Hard margarine (or butter), softened	1/4 cup	60 mL
Strawberry jam	2 tbsp.	30 mL
Strawberry jam	1/4 cup	60 mL

Cream margarine and brown sugar in large bowl. Add egg. Beat well. Add vanilla. Beat until smooth.

Combine next 4 ingredients in medium bowl. Add to margarine mixture in 2 additions, mixing well after each addition until no dry flour remains. Add coconut. Mix well. Roll into balls, using 2 tsp. (10 mL) dough for each. Arrange about 2 inches (5 cm) apart on greased cookie sheets. Flatten with lightly floured fork to 1/4 inch (6 mm) thickness. Bake in 375°F (190°C) oven for 7 to 10 minutes until edges are golden. Let stand on cookie sheets for 5 minutes before removing to wire racks to cool.

Strawberry Filling: Beat icing sugar and margarine in small bowl until smooth. Add first amount of jam. Beat well. Makes about 1/2 cup (125 mL) filling. Spread about 1 tsp. (5 mL) filling on bottom of 1/2 of cookies.

Spread about 1/2 tsp. (2 mL) second amount of jam on bottom of remaining cookies. Sandwich cookies, using 1 cookie with filling with 1 cookie with jam. Makes about 2 dozen (24) cookies.

1 cookie: 175 Calories; 9.7 g Total Fat (5.4 g Mono, 0.9 g Poly, 2.9 g Sat); 9 mg Cholesterol; 21 g Carbohydrate; 1 g Fibre; 2 g Protein; 171 mg Sodium

Pictured on page 81.

These fancy little meringues are perfect with your after-dinner coffee. Elegantly dipped in chocolate.

Coffee Meringues

Egg whites (large), room temperature	2	2
Cream of tartar	1/2 tsp.	2 mL
Granulated sugar	1/3 cup	75 mL
Icing (confectioner's) sugar	1/3 cup	75 mL
Instant coffee granules	1 tbsp.	15 mL
Warm water	1 tbsp.	15 mL
Semi-sweet chocolate baking squares (1 oz., 28 g, each), chopped	4	4

Beat egg whites and cream of tartar in medium bowl on medium until soft peaks form. Add granulated sugar 1 tbsp. (15 mL) at a time, beating constantly until stiff peaks form and sugar is dissolved. Fold in icing sugar.

Stir coffee granules into warm water in small cup until dissolved. Fold into meringue. Spoon meringue into piping bag fitted with large plain tip. Pipe 1 inch (2.5 cm) diameter mounds, lifting tip to create pointed end on each, about 2 inches (5 cm) apart onto parchment paper-lined cookie sheets. Bake on bottom rack in 225°F (110°C) oven for 35 to 40 minutes until dry. Turn oven off. Let stand in oven until cooled completely.

Heat chocolate in small heavy saucepan on lowest heat, stirring often until almost melted. Do not overheat. Remove from heat. Stir until smooth. Transfer to small custard cup. Dip each meringue halfway into chocolate, allowing excess to drip back into cup. Place on same parchment paper-lined cookie sheets. Let stand until set. Do not chill. Makes about 4 dozen (48) meringues.

1 meringue: 21 Calories; 0.7 g Total Fat (0.2 g Mono, 0 g Poly, 0.4 g Sat); 0 mg Cholesterol; 4 g Carbohydrate; trace Fibre; 0 g Protein; 3 mg Sodium

Pictured on page 85.

Cream cheese makes these oh, so soft!

note

Sanding sugar is a coarse decorating sugar that comes in white and various colours and is available at specialty kitchen stores.

Spritz

Hard margarine (or butter), softened	1 cup	250 mL
Granulated sugar	1 cup	250 mL
Block of cream cheese, softened	4 oz.	125 g
Large eggs	2	2
Vanilla	1 1/2 tsp.	7 mL
Salt	1/4 tsp.	1 mL

(continued on next page)

All-purpose flour	3 cups	750 mL

DECORATING SUGGESTIONS
Dragées
Glazed cherries
Granulated sugar
Sanding (decorating) sugar (see Note)

Cream margarine and sugar in large bowl. Add cream cheese. Beat well. Add eggs 1 at a time, beating well after each addition. Add vanilla and salt. Beat until smooth.

Add flour in 3 additions, mixing well after each addition until no dry flour remains. Fill cookie press with dough. Press your favourite design(s) about 2 inches (5 cm) apart onto ungreased cookie sheets.

Decorate cookies as desired. Bake in 350ºF (175ºC) oven for 10 to 12 minutes until edges are just golden. Let stand on cookie sheets for 5 minutes before removing to wire racks to cool. Makes about 8 dozen (96) cookies.

1 cookie: 48 Calories; 2.6 g Total Fat (1.5 g Mono, 0.3 g Poly, 0.7 g Sat); 6 mg Cholesterol; 5 g Carbohydrate; trace Fibre; 1 g Protein; 35 mg Sodium

Pictured below.

chocolate spritz

Replace 6 tbsp. (100 mL) of the flour with 6 tbsp. (100 mL) of sifted cocoa. Prepare and bake as directed.

orange spritz

Omit the vanilla. Use 1/2 tsp. (2 mL) orange flavouring plus 2 tsp. (10 mL) grated orange zest. Prepare and bake as directed.

Delicate meringues bonded together with delicious lemon filling. Greet your family with "kisses"—they will love you for it!

tip

To easily fill a piping bag, set it point-down in a large glass. Fold the top of the bag over the top of the glass like a cuff. Spoon the mixture into the bag.

Lemon Meringue Kisses

LEMON FILLING

Water	1 tbsp.	15 mL
Cornstarch	1 1/2 tsp.	7 mL
Egg yolks (large)	2	2
Granulated sugar	1/4 cup	60 mL
Lemon juice	1/4 cup	60 mL
Hard margarine (or butter), cut up	1/4 cup	60 mL
Grated lemon zest	1 1/2 tsp.	7 mL

MERINGUE KISSES

Egg whites (large)	2	2
Cream of tartar	1/2 tsp.	2 mL
Granulated sugar	1/3 cup	75 mL
Icing (confectioner's) sugar	1/3 cup	75 mL

Lemon Filling: Stir water into cornstarch in small cup until smooth. Set aside.

Combine egg yolks and sugar in small heavy saucepan. Add lemon juice and margarine. Heat and stir on medium-low for 1 to 2 minutes until margarine is melted. Stir cornstarch mixture. Add to lemon mixture. Heat and stir for about 1 minute until boiling and slightly thickened. Remove from heat.

Add lemon zest. Stir. Transfer to small bowl. Cover with plastic wrap, placing it directly on surface to prevent skin from forming. Chill for about 2 hours, stirring occasionally, until cold. Makes about 3/4 cup (175 mL) filling.

Meringue Kisses: Beat egg whites and cream of tartar in medium bowl on medium until soft peaks form.

Add granulated sugar 1 tbsp. (15 mL) at a time, beating constantly until stiff peaks form and sugar is dissolved.

(continued on next page)

Fold in icing sugar. Spoon meringue into piping bag fitted with large plain tip. Pipe 1/2 inch (12 mm) high by 1 inch (2.5 cm) diameter mounds, lifting tip to create pointed end on each, about 2 inches (5 cm) apart onto parchment paper-lined cookie sheets. Bake on bottom rack in 225°F (110°C) oven for about 45 minutes until dry. Turn oven off. Let stand in oven until cooled completely. Spoon lemon filling into separate piping bag fitted with plain medium tip. Pipe about 2 tsp. (10 mL) filling onto bottom of 1 meringue. Press bottom of second meringue onto filling. Repeat with remaining meringues and filling. Makes about 2 dozen (24) meringue kisses.

1 meringue kiss: 53 Calories; 2.5 g Total Fat (1.5 g Mono, 0.3 g Poly, 0.7 g Sat); 18 mg Cholesterol; 7 g Carbohydrate; 0 g Fibre; 1 g Protein; 29 mg Sodium

Pictured below.

Top: Lemon Meringue Kisses, page 84
Bottom: Coffee Meringues, page 82

Oodles of noodles make sweet, crunchy munchies! An old favourite.

kids in the kitchen

No-bake cookies are a great way to introduce children to cooking. They'll delight in making these types of treats themselves (with your help, of course).

Noodle Power

Semi-sweet chocolate chips	1 cup	250 mL
Butterscotch chips	1 cup	250 mL
Hard margarine (or butter)	1/4 cup	60 mL
Smooth peanut butter	1/4 cup	60 mL
Dry chow mein noodles	2 cups	500 mL
Unsalted peanuts	1 cup	250 mL

Heat first 4 ingredients in large heavy saucepan on lowest heat, stirring often until chocolate chips are almost melted. Do not overheat. Remove from heat. Stir until smooth.

Add noodles and peanuts. Stir until coated. Mixture will be soft. Drop, using 2 tsp. (10 mL) for each, onto waxed paper-lined cookie sheets. Let stand until set. May be chilled to speed setting. Makes about 3 dozen (36) cookies.

1 cookie: 102 Calories; 6.9 g Total Fat (3.1 g Mono, 1.6 g Poly, 1.8 g Sat); 0 mg Cholesterol; 10 g Carbohydrate; 1 g Fibre; 2 g Protein; 39 mg Sodium

Pictured on page 87.

Toffee with coffee—an afternoon treat.

Toffee Cookies

Bag of caramels (about 30)	9 1/2 oz.	269 g
Half-and-half cream	3 tbsp.	50 mL
Cornflakes cereal	2 cups	500 mL
Crisp rice cereal	1 cup	250 mL
Medium unsweetened coconut	1/2 cup	125 mL

Heat and stir caramels and cream in large saucepan on low for about 20 minutes until smooth. Remove from heat.

Add remaining 3 ingredients. Mix well. Drop, using 2 tsp. (10 mL) for each, onto greased cookie sheets. Let stand until set. May be chilled to speed setting. Makes about 3 1/2 dozen (42) cookies.

1 cookie: 41 Calories; 1.4 g Total Fat (0.1 g Mono, 0 g Poly, 1.1 g Sat); 1 mg Cholesterol; 7 g Carbohydrate; trace Fibre; 1 g Protein; 36 mg Sodium

Pictured on page 87.

Left: Toffee Cookies, above
Right: Noodle Power, this page

Make these whenever something sweet is in order. No cooking required!

pretty presentation

Nestle dipped or crumb-coated balls in small, decorative paper or foil baking cups to keep serving trays and fingers neat and clean.

Glazed Coffee Balls

Graham cracker crumbs	2 cups	500 mL
Icing (confectioner's) sugar	1/2 cup	125 mL
Finely chopped pecans	1/2 cup	125 mL
Hot water	1/2 cup	125 mL
Hard margarine (or butter)	2 tbsp.	30 mL
Instant coffee granules	1 tsp.	5 mL
COFFEE GLAZE		
Icing (confectioner's) sugar	3 cups	750 mL
Hard margarine (or butter), softened	3 tbsp.	50 mL
Cold prepared strong coffee	1/4 cup	60 mL

Finely chopped pecans (optional)

Combine graham crumbs, icing sugar and pecans in medium bowl.

Stir hot water, margarine and coffee granules in 2 cup (500 mL) liquid measure until margarine is melted and coffee granules are dissolved. Add to crumb mixture. Mix well. Roll into 1 inch (2.5 cm) balls. Place on waxed paper-lined cookie sheets.

Coffee Glaze: Beat first 3 ingredients in small bowl, adding more icing sugar or coffee if necessary until barely pourable consistency. Makes about 1 1/2 cups (375 mL) glaze. Place 1 ball on top of fork. Dip into glaze until coated. Place on same waxed paper-lined cookie sheet. Repeat with remaining balls and glaze.

Sprinkle with pecans. Let stand until set. May be chilled to speed setting. Makes about 3 dozen (36) balls.

1 ball: 111 Calories; 3.6 g Total Fat (2.2 g Mono, 1.4 g Poly, 0.6 g Sat); 0 mg Cholesterol; 20 g Carbohydrate; trace Fibre; 1 g Protein; 53 mg Sodium

Pictured on page 89.

A saucepan cookie for peanut fans. These won't last long.

Chocolate Peanut Drops

Granulated sugar	2 cups	500 mL
Milk	1/2 cup	125 mL
Hard margarine (or butter)	1/2 cup	125 mL
Cocoa, sifted if lumpy	6 tbsp.	100 mL
Smooth peanut butter	3/4 cup	175 mL
Vanilla	1 tsp.	5 mL
Quick-cooking rolled oats (not instant)	3 cups	750 mL
Chopped peanuts (or your favourite nuts), optional	1/2 cup	125 mL

Combine first 4 ingredients in medium saucepan. Bring to a boil on medium. Remove from heat.

Add peanut butter and vanilla. Stir until smooth. Add rolled oats and peanuts. Mix well. Let stand for 15 minutes. Working quickly, roll into small balls, using 1 tbsp. (15 mL) dough for each. Place on waxed paper-lined cookie sheets. Chill for 2 to 3 hours until firm. Makes about 5 dozen (60) cookies.

1 cookie: 84 Calories; 3.8 g Total Fat (2 g Mono, 0.8 g Poly, 0.8 g Sat); 0 mg Cholesterol; 12 g Carbohydrate; 1 g Fibre; 2 g Protein; 36 mg Sodium

Pictured on page 91.

Sweet and smooth, these taste like candy. Everyone's sure to think they're dandy!

Peanut Butter Chip Balls

Smooth peanut butter	1 cup	250 mL
Semi-sweet chocolate chips	1 cup	250 mL
Sweetened condensed milk	1/2 cup	125 mL
Icing (confectioner's) sugar	1/2 cup	125 mL

Combine all 4 ingredients in medium bowl. Roll into 1 inch (2.5 cm) balls. Place on waxed paper-lined cookie sheets. Chill for 2 to 3 hours until firm. Makes about 3 1/2 dozen (42) balls.

1 ball: 77 Calories; 4.9 g Total Fat (2.1 g Mono, 1 g Poly, 1.6 g Sat); 1 mg Cholesterol; 8 g Carbohydrate; 1 g Fibre; 2 g Protein; 36 mg Sodium

Pictured on page 91.

Top: Peanut Butter Chip tBalls, above
Bottom: Chocolate Peanut Drops, this page

These gently sweet treats are quick and easy to make.

note

To speed preparation, use a food processor to finely chop apricots and walnuts.

Apricot Balls

Medium unsweetened coconut	2 cups	500 mL
Very finely chopped dried apricot	1/2 lb.	225 g
Finely chopped walnuts (or your favourite nuts)	1/2 cup	125 mL
Sweetened condensed milk	1/2 cup	125 mL
Icing (confectioner's) sugar	1/4 cup	60 mL
Grated orange zest	1/2 tsp.	2 mL

Combine all 6 ingredients in medium bowl (see Note). Roll into 1 inch (2.5 cm) balls. Place on waxed paper-lined cookie sheets. Chill for 2 to 3 hours until firm. Makes about 5 dozen (60) balls.

1 ball: 47 Calories; 2.9 g Total Fat (0.3 g Mono, 0.5 g Poly, 2 g Sat); 1 mg Cholesterol; 5 g Carbohydrate; 1 g Fibre; 1 g Protein; 5 mg Sodium

Pictured on page 93.

Keep some of these on hand in the freezer for unexpected company. They'll be glad you did!

Cream Cheese Balls

Block of cream cheese, softened	8 oz.	250 g
Icing (confectioner's) sugar	1 cup	250 mL
Medium unsweetened coconut	1 cup	250 mL
Finely chopped maraschino cherries	1/3 cup	75 mL
Finely crushed vanilla wafers (about 80 wafers)	3 cups	750 mL
Can of crushed pineapple, drained	14 oz.	398 mL
GRAHAM CRACKER COATING		
Hard margarine (or butter)	2 tbsp.	30 mL
Graham cracker crumbs	3/4 cup	175 mL
Granulated sugar	1 tbsp.	15 mL

Beat cream cheese and icing sugar in large bowl until smooth. Add coconut and cherries. Stir.

Add crushed wafers and pineapple. Mix well. Cover. Chill for about 30 minutes until firm. Roll into 1 inch (2.5 cm) balls. Place on waxed paper-lined cookie sheets.

(continued on next page)

Graham Cracker Coating: Melt margarine in small saucepan on medium. Remove from heat. Add graham crumbs and sugar. Mix well. Roll balls in crumb mixture until coated. Place on same waxed paper-lined cookie sheet. Chill for 2 to 3 hours until firm. Makes about 7 dozen (84) balls.

1 ball: 46 Calories; 2.6 g Total Fat (0.7 g Mono, 0.2 g Poly, 1.5 g Sat); 5 mg Cholesterol; 5 g Carbohydrate; trace Fibre; 1 g Protein; 27 mg Sodium

Pictured below.

Left: Cream Cheese Balls, page 92
Right: Apricot Balls, page 92

Crisp, crunchy treats for the kid in each of us. Fabulous!

note

If chocolate becomes too thick for dipping, reheat on low until desired consistency.

Peanut Butter Balls

Smooth peanut butter	1 cup	250 mL
Icing (confectioner's) sugar	1 cup	250 mL
Hard margarine (or butter), softened	1 tbsp.	15 mL
Crisp rice cereal	1 cup	250 mL
Finely chopped walnuts	1/2 cup	125 mL
Chocolate melting wafers	2/3 cup	150 mL

Beat peanut butter, icing sugar and margarine in medium bowl until smooth.

Add cereal and walnuts. Mix well. Roll into 1 inch (2.5 cm) balls. Place on waxed paper-lined cookie sheets. Chill for 2 to 3 hours until firm.

Heat chocolate wafers in small heavy saucepan on lowest heat, stirring often until almost melted. Do not overheat. Remove from heat. Stir until smooth. Place 1 ball on fork. Dip into chocolate until coated, allowing excess to drip back into saucepan (see Note). Place on same waxed paper-lined cookie sheet. Repeat with remaining balls and chocolate. Let stand until set. May be chilled to speed setting. Makes about 4 1/2 dozen (54) balls.

1 ball: 62 Calories; 4.2 g Total Fat (1.7 g Mono, 1.2 g Poly, 1 g Sat); 0 mg Cholesterol; 5 g Carbohydrate; trace Fibre; 2 g Protein; 33 mg Sodium

Pictured on page 95.

The easiest recipe for first-time cooks to make. Maybe that's why this is such an old favourite! Simply delicious.

variation

Add a new twist to this classic cookie. Reduce the rolled oats to 1 1/2 cups (375 mL) and add 1 cup (250 mL) medium unsweetened coconut and 1/2 cup (125 mL) chopped glazed cherries.

Boiled Chocolate Cookies

Granulated sugar	2 cups	500 mL
Hard margarine (or butter)	1/2 cup	125 mL
Milk	1/2 cup	125 mL
Cocoa, sifted if lumpy	1/2 cup	125 mL
Quick-cooking rolled oats (not instant)	2 1/2 cups	625 mL

Combine first 4 ingredients in medium saucepan. Bring to a boil on medium. Reduce heat to medium-low. Simmer, uncovered, for 5 minutes, stirring occasionally. Remove from heat.

(continued on next page)

Add rolled oats. Mix well. Let stand for 15 minutes. Drop, using 1 tbsp. (15 mL) for each, onto waxed paper-lined cookie sheets. Chill for about 1 hour until firm. Makes about 5 1/2 dozen (66) cookies.

1 cookie: *56 Calories; 1.9 g Total Fat (1.1 g Mono, 0.3 g Poly, 0.4 g Sat); 0 mg Cholesterol; 10 g Carbohydrate; 1 g Fibre; 1 g Protein; 18 mg Sodium*

Pictured below.   Top: Boiled Chocolate Cookies, page 94
                                                   Bottom: Peanut Butter Balls, page 94

Laden with traditional Christmas ingredients, these will brighten any plate of goodies. Perfect for a cookie exchange.

tip

To keep logs of cookie dough from developing a flat side, turn them two or three times as they are chilling. Or, take a cardboard tube from a paper towel roll and cut it lengthwise. Put the wrapped log of cookie dough inside to maintain its round shape while chilling.

Merry Fruit Cookies

Coarsely chopped glazed cherries	2 cups	500 mL
Dark raisins	1 1/2 cups	375 mL
Chopped pitted dates	1 cup	250 mL
Red pineapple slices, cut up	4	4
Green pineapple slices, cut up	4	4
All-purpose flour	1/2 cup	125 mL
Hard margarine (or butter), softened	1 lb.	454 g
Granulated sugar	2 cups	500 mL
Large eggs	3	3
Vanilla	1 tsp.	5 mL
Almond flavouring	1/2 tsp.	2 mL
All-purpose flour	4 1/2 cups	1.1 L
Baking powder	1 tsp.	5 mL
Baking soda	1 tsp.	5 mL
Ground cinnamon	1/2 tsp.	2 mL

Put first 5 ingredients into large bowl. Add first amount of flour. Stir until fruit is coated.

Cream margarine and sugar in extra-large bowl. Add eggs 1 at a time, beating well after each addition. Add vanilla and flavouring. Beat until smooth.

Combine remaining 4 ingredients in separate large bowl. Add to margarine mixture in 3 additions, mixing well after each addition until no dry flour remains. Add fruit mixture. Mix well. Divide dough into 4 equal portions. Shape each portion into 10 inch (25 cm) long log. Wrap each log with waxed paper. Chill for at least 6 hours or overnight. Discard waxed paper from 1 log. Cut into 1/4 inch (6 mm) slices. Arrange about 2 inches (5 cm) apart on greased cookie sheets. Bake in 375°F (190°C) oven for about 10 minutes until golden. Let stand on cookie sheets for 5 minutes before removing to wire racks to cool. Repeat with remaining logs. Makes about 13 dozen (156) cookies.

1 cookie: *72 Calories; 2.5 g Total Fat (1.6 g Mono, 0.3 g Poly, 0.5 g Sat); 4 mg Cholesterol; 13 g Carbohydrate; trace Fibre; 1 g Protein; 40 mg Sodium*

Pictured on page 97.

Mmm... pretty much says it all!

Pictured on page 100.

tip

Using icing sugar instead of brown sugar will make a whiter shortbread with a slightly different texture. In this recipe, you can omit the brown sugar and increase the icing sugar to 3/4 cup (175 mL). Delicious either way!

note

Sanding sugar is a coarse decorating sugar that comes in white and various colours and is available at specialty kitchen stores.

variation

For a fancier presentation, roll out dough on lightly floured surface to 1/4 inch (6 mm) thickness and cut out shapes with lightly floured cookie cutter. Roll out scraps to cut more shapes. Bake as directed. Cool cookie sheets between batches so cookies retain their shape.

Shortbread

Butter (not margarine), softened	1 lb.	454 g
Brown sugar, packed (see Tip)	6 tbsp.	100 mL
Icing (confectioner's) sugar	6 tbsp.	100 mL
All-purpose flour	4 cups	1 L

DECORATING SUGGESTIONS
Sanding (decorating) sugar (see Note)
Glazed cherries, cut up
Candy sprinkles

Cream butter and both sugars in large bowl.

Add flour in 3 additions, mixing well after each addition until no dry flour remains. Knead dough in bowl if necessary to incorporate flour. Divide dough into 4 equal portions. Shape each portion into 6 inch (15 cm) long log. Wrap each log with waxed paper. Chill for at least 6 hours or overnight. Discard waxed paper from 1 log. Cut into 1/3 inch (1 cm) slices. Arrange about 2 inches (5 cm) apart on ungreased cookie sheets.

Decorate slices as desired. Bake in 325°F (160°C) oven for 12 to 15 minutes until edges are golden. Let stand on cookie sheets for 5 minutes before removing to wire racks to cool. Repeat with remaining logs. Makes about 8 dozen (96) cookies.

1 cookie: 59 Calories; 3.9 g Total Fat (1.1 g Mono, 0.2 g Poly, 2.4 g Sat); 10 mg Cholesterol; 6 g Carbohydrate; trace Fibre; 1 g Protein; 40 mg Sodium

Nutty Cherry Shortbread

Butter (not margarine), softened	1 lb.	454 g
Brown sugar, packed	2 cups	500 mL
All-purpose flour	3 1/2 cups	875 mL
Cornstarch	1/2 cup	125 mL
Coarsely chopped glazed cherries	1 cup	250 mL
Ground (or finely chopped) almonds	1 cup	250 mL

Cream butter and brown sugar in large bowl.

Combine flour and cornstarch in medium bowl. Add to butter mixture in 3 additions, mixing well after each addition until no dry flour remains. Knead dough in bowl if necessary to incorporate flour mixture.

Add cherries and almonds. Mix well. Divide dough into 4 equal portions. Shape each portion into 8 inch (20 cm) long log. Wrap each log with waxed paper. Chill for at least 6 hours or overnight. Discard waxed paper from 1 log. Cut into 1/4 inch (6 mm) slices. Arrange about 2 inches (5 cm) apart on ungreased cookie sheets. Bake in 375°F (190°C) oven for about 8 minutes until just golden. Let stand on cookie sheets for 5 minutes before removing to wire racks to cool. Repeat with remaining logs. Makes about 10 dozen (120) cookies.

1 cookie: 67 Calories; 3.4 g Total Fat (1.1 g Mono, 0.2 g Poly, 1.9 g Sat); 8 mg Cholesterol; 9 g Carbohydrate; trace Fibre; 1 g Protein; 33 mg Sodium

Pictured on pages 100/101.

There's no reason why shortbread can't dress up a bit for the holidays! A nice change from the ordinary.

Photo legend, next page

1. Nutty Cherry Shortbread, this page
2. Shortbread, page 98
3. Rolled Chocolate Shortbread, page 102
4. Whipped Shortbread, page 102

The chocolate you love in a buttery cookie. Yum.

variation

Enjoy the same great taste without fussing with cookie cutters! Shape each dough portion into 6 inch (15 cm) long log. Wrap each log with waxed paper. Chill for at least 6 hours or overnight. Discard waxed paper from 1 log. Cut into 1/4 inch (6 mm) slices. Bake as directed. Repeat with remaining log.

Rolled Chocolate Shortbread

Butter (not margarine), softened	1 cup	250 mL
Icing (confectioner's) sugar	1/2 cup	125 mL
Cocoa, sifted if lumpy	1/4 cup	60 mL
All-purpose flour	1 3/4 cups	425 mL

Beat butter and icing sugar in large bowl until smooth. Add cocoa. Beat well.

Add flour in 2 additions, mixing well after each addition until no dry flour remains. Knead dough in bowl if necessary to incorporate flour. Divide dough into 2 equal portions. Roll out each portion on lightly floured surface to 1/4 inch (6 mm) thickness. Cut out shapes with lightly floured 2 3/4 inch (7 cm) cookie cutters. Roll out scraps to cut more shapes. Arrange about 2 inches (5 cm) apart on ungreased cookie sheets. Bake in 325°F (160°C) oven for about 12 minutes until firm. Let stand on cookie sheets for 5 minutes before removing to wire racks to cool. Cool cookie sheets between batches. Repeat with remaining dough portion. Makes about 3 dozen (36) cookies.

1 cookie: 79 Calories; 5.6 g Total Fat (1.6 g Mono, 0.2 g Poly, 3.4 g Sat); 15 mg Cholesterol; 7 g Carbohydrate; trace Fibre; 1 g Protein; 55 mg Sodium

Pictured on page 101.

Melt-in-your-mouth goodness you'll crave year-round.

an added touch

For a bit of sparkle, sprinkle cookies with granulated sugar or sanding (decorating) sugar before baking. Sanding sugar is a coarse decorating sugar that comes in white and various colours and is available at specialty kitchen stores.

Whipped Shortbread

Butter (not margarine), softened	1 cup	250 mL
Granulated sugar	1/2 cup	125 mL
All-purpose flour	1 1/2 cups	375 mL
Cornstarch	1/4 cup	60 mL
Maraschino cherries, halved and blotted dry (optional)	18	18

Beat butter and sugar in medium bowl for about 5 minutes until light and creamy.

(continued on next page)

Combine flour and cornstarch in small bowl. Add to butter mixture in 2 additions, beating well after each addition until no dry flour remains. Drop, using 1 tbsp. (15 mL) for each, about 2 inches (5 cm) apart onto ungreased cookie sheets.

If desired, put 1 cherry half in centre of each cookie. Bake in 375°F (190°C) oven for about 12 minutes until edges are just golden. Let stand on cookie sheets for 5 minutes before removing to wire racks to cool. Makes about 3 dozen (36) cookies.

1 cookie: 86 Calories; 5.9 g Total Fat (1.9 g Mono, 0.3 g Poly, 3.4 g Sat); 15 mg Cholesterol; 7 g Carbohydrate; trace Fibre; 1 g Protein; 56 mg Sodium

Pictured on page 101.

Chewy Cookie Clusters

Cornflakes cereal	3 cups	750 mL
Golden raisins	1 1/2 cups	375 mL
Shelled pistachios, toasted (see Note)	1 1/2 cups	375 mL
Sliced almonds, toasted (see Note)	1 cup	250 mL
Chopped red glazed cherries	1 cup	250 mL
Grated orange zest	1/2 tsp.	2 mL
Can of sweetened condensed milk	11 oz.	300 mL
Hard margarine (or butter), melted	2 tbsp.	30 mL

Combine first 6 ingredients in large bowl.

Add condensed milk and margarine. Mix well. Drop, using 2 tbsp. (30 mL) for each, about 2 inches (5 cm) apart onto parchment paper-lined cookie sheets. Bake in 350°F (175°C) oven for about 8 minutes until golden. Let stand on cookie sheets for 5 minutes before removing to wire racks to cool. Makes about 4 dozen (48) cookies.

1 cookie: 104 Calories; 4.7 g Total Fat (2.8 g Mono, 0.7 g Poly, 1 g Sat); 3 mg Cholesterol; 15 g Carbohydrate; 1 g Fibre; 2 g Protein; 33 mg Sodium

Pictured on page 105.

An assortment of tasty tidbits makes colourful clusters for tea time.

note

To toast nuts, spread them evenly in an ungreased shallow pan. Bake in a 350°F (175°C) oven for 5 to 10 minutes, stirring or shaking often, until desired doneness.

So not everyone loves fruitcake, but these are so good they might just change someone's mind!

Fruitcake Cookies

Mixed glazed fruit	2 cups	500 mL
Raisins	1 cup	250 mL
Chopped pitted dates	1 cup	250 mL
Chopped pecans	1 cup	250 mL
All-purpose flour	1/2 cup	125 mL
Hard margarine (or butter), softened	1/2 cup	125 mL
Granulated sugar	1 cup	250 mL
Large eggs	2	2
Vanilla	1 tsp.	5 mL
All-purpose flour	1 cup	250 mL
Baking soda	1/2 tsp.	2 mL
Ground cinnamon (optional)	1/4 tsp.	1 mL

Put first 4 ingredients into large bowl. Add first amount of flour. Stir until fruit is coated.

Cream margarine and sugar in separate large bowl. Add eggs 1 at a time, beating well after each addition. Add vanilla. Beat until smooth.

Combine second amount of flour, baking soda and cinnamon in small bowl. Add to margarine mixture. Mix until no dry flour remains. Add fruit mixture. Mix well. Drop, using 1 1/2 tbsp. (25 mL) for each, about 2 inches (5 cm) apart onto greased cookie sheets. Bake in 325°F (160°C) oven for 15 to 18 minutes until golden. Remove to wire racks to cool. Makes about 5 dozen (60) cookies.

1 cookie: 96 Calories; 3.3 g Total Fat (2 g Mono, 0.6 g Poly, 0.5 g Sat); 7 mg Cholesterol; 17 g Carbohydrate; 1 g Fibre; 1 g Protein; 37 mg Sodium

Pictured on page 105.

In cup: Fruitcake Cookies, above
On saucer: Chewy Cookie Clusters, page 103

Pretty cookies to accent a plate of sweets.

note

To toast coconut and nuts, spread them evenly in separate ungreased shallow pans. Bake in a 350°F (175°C) oven for 5 to 10 minutes, stirring or shaking often, until desired doneness.

Striped Corners

Hard margarine (or butter), softened	1 cup	250 mL
Icing (confectioner's) sugar	1 1/2 cups	375 mL
Large egg	1	1
All-purpose flour	3 cups	750 mL
Salt	1/4 tsp.	1 mL
Irish cream-flavoured powdered coffee whitener	1/3 cup	75 mL
Cocoa, sifted if lumpy	1 tbsp.	15 mL
Flake coconut, toasted (see Note)	2/3 cup	150 mL
Chopped sliced almonds, toasted (see Note)	2/3 cup	150 mL
Milk chocolate chips	1 cup	250 mL

Beat margarine and icing sugar in large bowl until smooth. Add egg. Beat well.

Combine flour and salt in medium bowl. Add to margarine mixture in 3 additions, mixing well after each addition until no dry flour remains. Divide dough into 2 equal portions.

Add coffee whitener and cocoa to 1 portion. Mix until evenly coloured. Shape into 16 inch (40 cm) long log. Flatten slightly. Shape remaining portion into 16 inch (40 cm) long log. Flatten slightly. Wrap each portion with plastic wrap. Chill for 2 hours. Discard plastic wrap from 1 portion. Roll out between 2 sheets of waxed paper to 4 x 24 inch (10 x 60 cm) rectangle. Repeat with remaining portion. Discard top sheet of waxed paper from both rectangles. Flip 1 rectangle onto the other, aligning edges of dough as evenly as possible. Press together. Discard top sheet of waxed paper. Roll up tightly from short side, jelly roll-style, using waxed paper as a guide. Roll should be about 3 1/2 inches (9 cm) in diameter. Wrap tightly with same sheet of waxed paper. Chill for at least 6 hours or overnight. Discard waxed paper. Cut into 1/4 inch (6 mm) slices. Cut each slice into 4 wedges. Arrange about 2 inches (5 cm) apart on ungreased cookie sheets. Bake in 400°F (205°C) oven for about 7 minutes until edges are just golden. Let stand on cookie sheets for 5 minutes before removing to wire racks to cool. Cool cookie sheets between batches.

(continued on next page)

Combine coconut and almonds in small dish. Heat chocolate chips in small heavy saucepan on lowest heat, stirring often until almost melted. Do not overheat. Remove from heat. Stir until smooth. Dip curved edge of each cookie in chocolate, then immediately into coconut mixture. Place on waxed paper-lined cookie sheet. Let stand until set. Makes about 5 1/2 dozen (66) cookies.

1 cookie: *92 Calories; 5.4 g Total Fat (2.7 g Mono, 0.5 g Poly, 1.9 g Sat); 4 mg Cholesterol;*
10 g Carbohydrate; trace Fibre; 1 g Protein; 48 mg Sodium

Pictured below.

Watch their eyes sparkle with delight when you bring these to the table!

Mocha Diamonds

Hard margarine (or butter), softened	1 1/2 cups	375 mL
Brown sugar, packed	1 1/2 cups	375 mL
Instant coffee granules, crushed to fine powder	1 1/2 tsp.	7 mL
Almond flavouring	1 1/2 tsp.	7 mL
All-purpose flour	3 1/3 cups	825 mL
Baking powder	3/4 tsp.	4 mL
Salt	1/2 tsp.	2 mL
Milk chocolate bars (3 1/2 oz., 100 g, each), finely chopped	3	3
Chopped sliced almonds	3/4 cup	175 mL

Cream margarine and brown sugar in large bowl. Add coffee granules and flavouring. Beat until smooth.

Combine flour, baking powder and salt in medium bowl. Add to margarine mixture in 3 additions, mixing well after each addition until no dry flour remains.

Add chocolate and almonds. Mix well. Line greased 11 x 17 inch (28 x 43 cm) baking sheet with sides with parchment (not waxed) paper, extending paper 2 inches (5 cm) over long sides. Press dough evenly in baking sheet. Place sheet of waxed paper on top. Roll evenly with rolling pin. Discard waxed paper. Bake in 325°F (160°C) oven for about 30 minutes until golden. Let stand in baking sheet on wire rack for 20 minutes. While still warm, make 10 evenly spaced cuts lengthwise about 1 inch (2.5 cm) apart. Cut diagonally across lengthwise cuts to create small diamond shapes (see Note). Let stand in baking sheet on wire rack until cooled completely. Holding parchment paper, remove from pan. Re-cut if necessary. Discard parchment paper. Makes about 11 dozen (132) cookies.

1 cookie: *57 Calories; 3.3 g Total Fat (1.9 g Mono, 0.3 g Poly, 0.9 g Sat); 1 mg Cholesterol; 7 g Carbohydrate; trace Fibre; 1 g Protein; 40 mg Sodium*

Pictured on page 109.

Brimming with an assortment of fruit and nuts, these cookies are the perfect choice to announce the arrival of the holiday season.

Christmas Cookies

Hard margarine (or butter), softened	1 cup	250 mL
Brown sugar, packed	3/4 cup	175 mL
Large egg	1	1
All-purpose flour	1 1/4 cups	300 mL
Baking soda	1/2 tsp.	2 mL
Ground cinnamon	1/2 tsp.	2 mL
Salt	1/2 tsp.	2 mL
Chopped walnuts	1 cup	250 mL
Chopped Brazil nuts	1/2 cup	125 mL
Slivered almonds	1/2 cup	125 mL
Chopped pitted dates	1/2 cup	125 mL
Chopped glazed cherries	1/2 cup	125 mL
Glazed pineapple slices, chopped	2	2

Cream margarine and brown sugar in large bowl. Add egg. Beat well.

Combine next 4 ingredients in medium bowl. Add to margarine mixture. Mix until no dry flour remains.

Add remaining 6 ingredients. Mix well. Drop, using 1 1/2 tbsp. (25 mL) for each, about 2 inches (5 cm) apart onto greased cookie sheets. Bake in 350°F (175°C) oven for 10 to 12 minutes until golden. Remove to wire racks to cool. Makes about 4 dozen (48) cookies.

1 cookie: 112 Calories; 7.5 g Total Fat (3.9 g Mono, 2 g Poly, 1.3 g Sat); 4 mg Cholesterol; 10 g Carbohydrate; 1 g Fibre; 2 g Protein; 88 mg Sodium

Pictured on page 111.

Extra-special cookies for extra-special occasions. When only the best will do, these are sure to impress!

Cranberry Macadamia Mounds

Ingredient	Imperial	Metric
Dried cranberries	1 1/2 cups	375 mL
Orange juice	1/2 cup	125 mL
Orange-flavoured liqueur (such as Grand Marnier)	2 tbsp.	30 mL
All-purpose flour	3 cups	750 mL
Brown sugar, packed	1 1/2 cups	375 mL
White chocolate chips	1 cup	250 mL
Coarsely chopped macadamia nuts, toasted (see Note)	1 cup	250 mL
Baking powder	1 1/2 tbsp.	25 mL
Salt	1/2 tsp.	2 mL
Large egg	1	1
Buttermilk (or reconstituted from powder)	1 cup	250 mL
Hard margarine (or butter), melted	2/3 cup	150 mL
Grated orange zest	1 tbsp.	15 mL

Combine first 3 ingredients in small bowl. Let stand for 30 minutes, stirring occasionally. Drain, reserving liquid if desired (see Serving Suggestion).

Combine next 6 ingredients in large bowl. Make a well in centre.

Beat remaining 4 ingredients with whisk in separate small bowl. Add to well. Add cranberries. Stir until just moistened. Drop, using 1 1/2 tbsp. (25 mL) for each, about 2 inches (5 cm) apart onto greased cookie sheets. Bake in 375°F (190°C) oven for 10 to 12 minutes until just golden and wooden pick inserted in centre of cookie comes out clean. Let stand on cookie sheets for 5 minutes before removing to wire racks to cool. Makes about 6 dozen (72) cookies.

1 cookie: 90 Calories; 4.2 g Total Fat (2.6 g Mono, 0.3 g Poly, 1.1 g Sat); 4 mg Cholesterol; 12 g Carbohydrate; 1 g Fibre; 1 g Protein; 70 mg Sodium

Pictured on page 113.

A versatile dough to bake into a variety of shapes. We've included a few suggestions below. Have fun!

cookie ornaments

Instead of circles, cut out festive shapes with an assortment of cookie cutters such as stars, Christmas trees and gingerbread men. Make a hole with a drinking straw about 1/2 inch (12 mm) from the top edge of each cookie before baking. Decorate with candies, sprinkles or Royal Icing, page 116. Tie ribbon through each hole for hanging.

lollipop cookies

Prepare dough as directed. Roll into balls, using 1/3 cup (75 mL) for each. With a flat-bottomed glass, press each ball on lightly floured surface to 1/4 inch (6 mm) thickness. Place 1 round on top of 5 inch (12.5 cm) lollipop stick, covering 1 to 1 1/2 inches (2.5 to 3.8 cm) of stick. Press dough lightly onto stick. Repeat with remaining rounds and sticks, arranging about 2 inches (5 cm) apart on greased cookie sheets, alternating direction of sticks. Bake in 350°F (175°C) oven for 8 to 10 minutes until firm. Let stand on cookie sheets for 5 minutes before removing to wire racks to cool.

Rolled Ginger Cookies

Hard margarine (or butter), softened	1/4 cup	60 mL
Granulated sugar	1/2 cup	125 mL
Fancy (mild) molasses	1/2 cup	125 mL
Water	1/3 cup	75 mL
All-purpose flour	3 1/4 cups	800 mL
Baking soda	1 tsp.	5 mL
Ground ginger	1 tsp.	5 mL
Salt	1/2 tsp.	2 mL
Ground cinnamon	1/2 tsp.	2 mL
Ground cloves	1/4 tsp.	1 mL
Golden corn syrup	2 tbsp.	30 mL
Assorted candies, for decorating		

Cream margarine and sugar in large bowl. Add molasses and water. Beat until smooth.

Combine next 6 ingredients in medium bowl. Add to margarine mixture in 3 additions, mixing well after each addition until no dry flour remains. Roll out dough on lightly floured surface to 1/4 inch (6 mm) thickness. Cut out circles with lightly floured 2 inch (5 cm) cookie cutter. Roll out scraps to cut more circles. Arrange about 2 inches (5 cm) apart on greased cookie sheets. Bake in 350°F (175°C) oven for 8 to 10 minutes until firm. Let stand on cookie sheets for 5 minutes before removing to wire racks to cool. Cool cookie sheets between batches.

Measure corn syrup into small custard cup set in small heatproof bowl. Pour boiling water into bowl until halfway up side of custard cup. Let stand until corn syrup is warm. Brush corn syrup with small paintbrush on top of each cookie. Decorate with candies as desired. Place on waxed paper-lined cookie sheets. Let stand until set. Makes about 2 dozen (24) cookies.

1 cookie: 125 Calories; 2.2 g Total Fat (1.3 g Mono, 0.3 g Poly, 0.5 g Sat); 0 mg Cholesterol; 24 g Carbohydrate; 1 g Fibre; 2 g Protein; 132 mg Sodium

Pictured on page 115.

A very good, versatile cookie. Cut out and decorate shapes appropriate for the occasion. For a fun birthday party activity, have the kids decorate them to take home as party favours.

an added touch

For a bit of sparkle, sprinkle cookies with granulated sugar or sanding (decorating) sugar before baking. Sanding sugar is a coarse decorating sugar that comes in white and various colours and is available at specialty kitchen stores.

royal icing

Beat 2 2/3 cups (650 mL) icing sugar, 1/4 cup (60 mL) water and 2 tbsp. (30 mL) meringue powder in large bowl on medium until stiff peaks form. Add food colouring, if desired. Spread icing on cookies and decorate with candy sprinkles or dragées. If preferred, spoon icing into piping bag fitted with small writing tip or into small resealable freezer bag with tiny piece snipped off corner. Pipe icing in decorative pattern onto cookies.

Sugar Cookies

Hard margarine (or butter), softened	3/4 cup	175 mL
Granulated sugar	3/4 cup	175 mL
Large egg	1	1
Vanilla	1 tsp.	5 mL
All-purpose flour	2 cups	500 mL
Baking soda	1 tsp.	5 mL
Cream of tartar	1 tsp.	5 mL
Salt	1/4 tsp.	1 mL
Ground cardamom (optional)	1/4 tsp.	1 mL

Cream margarine and sugar in large bowl. Add egg. Beat well. Add vanilla. Beat until smooth.

Combine remaining 5 ingredients in small bowl. Add to margarine mixture in 2 additions, mixing well after each addition until no dry flour remains. Divide dough into 2 equal portions. Shape each portion into flattened disc. Wrap each with waxed paper. Chill for at least 6 hours or overnight. Discard waxed paper from 1 disc. Roll out dough on lightly floured surface to 1/8 inch (3 mm) thickness. Cut out circles with lightly floured 2 inch (5 cm) cookie cutter. Roll out scraps to cut more circles. Arrange about 2 inches (5 cm) apart on greased cookie sheets. Bake in 350°F (175°C) oven for about 10 minutes until edges are just golden. Let stand on cookie sheets for 5 minutes before removing to wire racks to cool. Cool cookie sheets between batches. Repeat with remaining disc. Decorate with Royal Icing, if desired. Makes about 7 dozen (84) cookies.

1 cookie: 35 Calories; 1.8 g Total Fat (1.2 g Mono, 0.2 g Poly, 0.4 g Sat); 3 mg Cholesterol; 4 g Carbohydrate; trace Fibre; 0 g Protein; 43 mg Sodium

Pictured on page 117.

Serve these Jack-O'-Lanterns at your next Halloween party. They're sure to be a smash!

note

Paste food colouring makes a bolder colour than liquid food colouring and is the best choice for these cookies in order to avoid thinning dough.

raisin sandwich cookies

Omit the food colouring. Instead of jack-o'-lantern faces, make a design of your choice using a knife or a small cookie cutter. Bake as directed.

Jack-O'-Lantern Cookies

RAISIN FILLING

Chopped dark raisins	1 1/2 cups	375 mL
Water	1/2 cup	125 mL
Granulated sugar	1/4 cup	60 mL
Hard margarine (or butter)	2 tsp.	10 mL
Lemon juice	2 tsp.	10 mL
Salt, sprinkle		
Hard margarine (or butter), softened	1 cup	250 mL
Granulated sugar	1 1/4 cups	300 mL
Large eggs	2	2
Milk	1 tbsp.	15 mL
Vanilla	1 tsp.	5 mL
All-purpose flour	2 cups	500 mL
Whole wheat flour	2/3 cup	150 mL
Baking powder	2 tsp.	10 mL
Salt	1/2 tsp.	2 mL
Ground cardamom	1/4 tsp.	1 mL

Orange paste food colouring (see Note)

Raisin Filling: Combine first 6 ingredients in medium saucepan. Bring to a boil on medium, stirring occasionally. Reduce heat to low. Simmer, uncovered, for 10 to 12 minutes, stirring occasionally, until thickened. Cool. Makes about 1 1/4 cup (300 mL) filling.

Cream second amounts of margarine and sugar in large bowl. Add eggs 1 at a time, beating well after each addition. Add milk and vanilla. Beat until smooth.

Combine next 5 ingredients in medium bowl. Add to margarine mixture in 2 additions, mixing well after each addition until no dry flour remains.

Add food colouring, a small amount at a time, kneading dough in bowl until colour is even and dough is bright orange. Divide into 2 equal portions. Shape each portion into flattened disc. Wrap each with waxed paper. Chill for at least 6 hours or overnight. Discard waxed paper from 1 disc. Roll out dough on lightly floured surface to 1/8 inch (3 mm) thickness. Cut out circles with lightly floured 2 1/2 inch (6.4 cm) round cookie cutter. Roll out scraps to cut more circles. Use knife to cut out faces on 1/2 of circles (see photo, page 120).

(continued on next page)

Spread about 1 1/2 tsp. (7 mL) filling on each whole circle, leaving 1/4 inch (6 mm) edge. Place faces on top of filling. Press edges together with fork to seal. Arrange about 2 inches (5 cm) apart on ungreased cookie sheets. Bake in 375°F (190°C) oven for 10 to 12 minutes until firm. Let stand on cookie sheets for 5 minutes before removing to wire racks to cool. Repeat with remaining disc and filling. Makes about 3 dozen (36) cookies.

1 cookie: 143 Calories; 6 g Total Fat (3.8 g Mono, 0.7 g Poly, 1.3 g Sat); 12 mg Cholesterol; 21 g Carbohydrate; 1 g Fibre; 2 g Protein; 124 mg Sodium

Pictured on page 120.

Almond Finger Cookies

Vegetable shortening (or lard), softened	1 cup	250 mL
Granulated sugar	1 cup	250 mL
Large egg	1	1
Almond flavouring	2 tsp.	10 mL
All-purpose flour	2 1/2 cups	625 mL
Baking powder	1 1/2 tsp.	7 mL
Salt	1/4 tsp.	1 mL
Ground almonds	3/4 cup	175 mL
Whole blanched almonds	48	48

Cream shortening and sugar in large bowl. Add egg and flavouring. Beat well.

Combine flour, baking powder and salt in medium bowl. Add to shortening mixture in 3 additions, mixing well after each addition until no dry flour remains. Knead dough in bowl until smooth.

Add ground almonds. Mix well. Divide dough into 8 equal portions. Divide each portion into 6 pieces. Shape each piece into 3 inch (7.5 cm) long log or finger. Arrange about 2 inches (5 cm) apart on greased cookie sheets. Squeeze each finger in centre to form knuckle. Press 1 whole almond on 1 end of each finger to form nail. Bake in 350°F (175°C) oven for 10 to 13 minutes until firm. Let stand on cookie sheets for 5 minutes before removing to wire racks to cool. Makes 4 dozen (48) cookies.

1 cookie: 97 Calories; 5.8 g Total Fat (2.7 g Mono, 1.2 g Poly, 1.3 g Sat); 4 mg Cholesterol; 10 g Carbohydrate; trace Fibre; 1 g Protein; 26 mg Sodium

Pictured on page 121.

Let these point the way to party fun. Sensationally spooky and good for a laugh—a Halloween howl, you might say.

witch's fingers

Knead green food colouring into dough until desired shade is reached. Use paste food colouring to make a bolder colour. Use only a few drops of liquid food colouring to make a softer colour. Prepare and bake as directed. For coloured nails, soak whole almonds for 30 minutes in a mixture of 1/4 cup (60 mL) water and 1/8 tsp. (0.5 mL) red or green paste food colouring. Let dry.

Pictured on page 121.

Photo legend, next page
Left: Jack-O'-Lantern Cookies, page 118
Right: Almond Finger Cookies, this page
and Witch's Fingers, above

And you thought monsters only hid under the bed! Find some friendly ones peeking out from these whimsical, cake-like treats. Great for a birthday or Halloween party.

halloween black moons

Omit the chocolate pudding powder and candies. Use the same package size of vanilla pudding powder plus enough orange paste food colouring to make the filling a bright orange. Spread between cookie halves as directed.

Pictured on page 123.

Mud Monsters

Hard margarine (or butter), softened	1/2 cup	125 mL
Granulated sugar	1 cup	250 mL
Cocoa, sifted if lumpy	1/2 cup	125 mL
Large eggs	2	2
Vanilla	1 tsp.	5 mL
All-purpose flour	2 cups	500 mL
Baking soda	1 1/2 tsp.	7 mL
Baking powder	1/2 tsp.	2 mL
Salt	1/2 tsp.	2 mL
Milk	1 cup	250 mL

COOL CHOCOLATE FILLING

Envelopes of dessert topping (not prepared)	2	2
Box of instant chocolate pudding powder (4 serving size)	1	1
Cold milk	1 1/2 cups	375 mL

Assorted candies, for decorating

Cream margarine and sugar in large bowl. Add cocoa. Beat well. Add eggs 1 at a time, beating well after each addition. Add vanilla. Beat well.

Combine next 4 ingredients in medium bowl. Add to margarine mixture in 3 additions, alternating with milk in 2 additions, beginning and ending with flour mixture, beating well after each addition. Drop, using 3 tbsp. (50 mL) for each, about 4 inches (10 cm) apart onto greased cookie sheets. Bake in 425°F (220°C) oven for about 10 minutes until puffed and firm. Let stand on cookie sheets for 5 minutes before removing to wire racks to cool completely.

Cool Chocolate Filling: Beat dessert topping, pudding powder and cold milk in separate large bowl for about 5 minutes until spreading consistency. Makes 2 2/3 cups (650 mL) filling. Slice each cookie in half horizontally. Spread 2 tbsp. (30 mL) filling on bottom half of each cookie. Cover with top halves. Press each cookie gently until small amount of filling oozes out between layers.

Press candies into filling to create "monster" faces (see photo). Makes about 2 dozen (24) cookies.

1 cookie: 170 Calories; 6.6 g Total Fat (3 g Mono, 0.6 g Poly, 2.6 g Sat); 19 mg Cholesterol; 26 g Carbohydrate; 1 g Fibre; 3 g Protein; 276 mg Sodium

Pictured on page 123.

Top left: Halloween Black Moons, this page
Bottom right: Mud Monsters, above

Throughout this book measurements are given in Conventional and Metric measure. To compensate for differences between the two measurements due to rounding, a full metric measure is not always used. The cup used is the standard 8 fluid ounce. Temperature is given in degrees Fahrenheit and Celsius. Baking pan measurements are in inches and centimetres as well as quarts and litres. An exact metric conversion is given on this page as well as the working equivalent (Metric Standard Measure).

Pans

Conventional – Inches	Metric – Centimetres
8 x 8 inch	20 x 20 cm
9 x 9 inch	22 x 22 cm
9 x 13 inch	22 x 33 cm
10 x 15 inch	25 x 38 cm
11 x 17 inch	28 x 43 cm
8 x 2 inch round	20 x 5 cm
9 x 2 inch round	22 x 5 cm
10 x 4 1/2 inch tube	25 x 11 cm
8 x 4 x 3 inch loaf	20 x 10 x 7.5 cm
9 x 5 x 3 inch loaf	22 x 12.5 x 7.5 cm

Oven Temperatures

Fahrenheit (°F)	Celsius (°C)	Fahrenheit (°F)	Celsius (°C)
175°	80°	350°	175°
200°	95°	375°	190°
225°	110°	400°	205°
250°	120°	425°	220°
275°	140°	450°	230°
300°	150°	475°	240°
325°	160°	500°	260°

Spoons

Conventional Measure	Metric Exact Conversion Millilitre (mL)	Metric Standard Measure Millilitre (mL)
1/8 teaspoon (tsp.)	0.6 mL	0.5 mL
1/4 teaspoon (tsp.)	1.2 mL	1 mL
1/2 teaspoon (tsp.)	2.4 mL	2 mL
1 teaspoon (tsp.)	4.7 mL	5 mL
2 teaspoons (tsp.)	9.4 mL	10 mL
1 tablespoon (tbsp.)	14.2 mL	15 mL

Cups

1/4 cup (4 tbsp.)	56.8 mL	60 mL
1/3 cup (5 1/3 tbsp.)	75.6 mL	75 mL
1/2 cup (8 tbsp.)	113.7 mL	125 mL
2/3 cup (10 2/3 tbsp.)	151.2 mL	150 mL
3/4 cup (12 tbsp.)	170.5 mL	175 mL
1 cup (16 tbsp.)	227.3 mL	250 mL
4 1/2 cups	1022.9 mL	1000 mL(1 L)

Dry Measurements

Conventional Measure Ounces (oz.)	Metric Exact Conversion Grams (g)	Metric Standard Measure Grams (g)
1 oz.	28.3 g	28 g
2 oz.	56.7 g	57 g
3 oz.	85.0 g	85 g
4 oz.	113.4 g	125 g
5 oz.	141.7 g	140 g
6 oz.	170.1 g	170 g
7 oz.	198.4 g	200 g
8 oz.	226.8 g	250 g
16 oz.	453.6 g	500 g
32 oz.	907.2 g	1000 g (1 kg)

Casseroles

Canada & Britain		United States	
Standard Size Casserole	Exact Metric Measure	Standard Size Casserole	Exact Metric Measure
1 qt. (5 cups)	1.13 L	1 qt. (4 cups)	900 mL
1 1/2 qts. (7 1/2 cups)	1.69 L	1 1/2 qts. (6 cups)	1.35 L
2 qts. (10 cups)	2.25 L	2 qts. (8 cups)	1.8 L
2 1/2 qts. (12 1/2 cups)	2.81 L	2 1/2 qts. (10 cups)	2.25 L
3 qts. (15 cups)	3.38 L	3 qts. (12 cups)	2.7 L
4 qts. (20 cups)	4.5 L	4 qts. (16 cups)	3.6 L
5 qts. (25 cups)	5.63 L	5 qts. (20 cups)	4.5 L

Tip Index

Recipe Index

most loved recipe collection most loved recipe collection